Surfcaster's Quest

Books by Roy Rowan

The Four Days of Mayaguez
The Intuitive Manager
A Day in the Life of Italy (coeditor)
Powerful People
First Dogs
Surfcaster's Quest

SURFCASTER'S QUEST

Seeking Stripers, Blues, and Solitude at the Edge of the Surging Sea

ROY ROWAN

THE LYONS PRESS

Printed in the United States of America
10 9 8 7 6 5 4 3 2 1

Library of Congresss Cataloging-in-Publication Data
Rowan, Roy.
Surfcaster's quest : seeking stripers, blues, and solitude
at the edge of the surging sea / Roy Rowan.
p. cm.
ISBN 1-55821-981-1 (hc.)
1. Surf casting—Rhode Island—Block Island Anecdotes.
2. Rowan, Roy. I. Title.
SH454.7 .R68 1999
799.1'66146—dc21   99-32030
                                                                  CIP

CONTENTS

1

Getting Hooked

*"Man is a rope stretched between the animal
and the Superman—a rope over an abyss."*
Friedrich Wilhelm Nietzsche (1844–1900),
Thus Spake Zarathustra

Anyone who has never battled a bull striper all alone on a beach may not understand the closeness it's possible to feel to a fish. The instinctual strand that can bind a human and an animal doesn't stem simply from the striper's enormous size. Or even from the fierceness of the fight coming from the other end of the line. The connection is more obscure, born out of respect for a creature that has eluded net, spear, and hook for fifteen or even twenty years.

· 1 ·

After the initial electrifying jolt—a strike so hard and unexpected the rod almost flies from your hands—comes a primordial message from your quarry, as clear and challenging as any emanating from a human mouth. Only this message is passed through the pulsating monofilament line, into your two hands, up through your arms and neck and directly into your brain. Its meaning, nevertheless, is brutally clear.

"You and I, Mr. Fisherman, though temporarily tied together, are engaged in a deadly duel of endurance that only one of us can win." Right away you're aware of the striper's vast capacity for courage and determined will to live, the same powers that propel people through a long and successful life.

The strange sensation of closeness felt with this fish is amplified by the fact that no other human is there to intrude on the battle. No fellow fisherman around to shout advice or encouragement. No beach walker strolling idly by to stop and watch if you win or lose. And most important of all, no tenderhearted preservationist present to suggest releasing your prize, if it's ever yours to let go.

As the big bass strips off line, swimming furiously to break free and spit out the unchewable plastic minnow hooked in its mouth, a single thought seizes your mind: "Can I stop this fish's surge before it snaps my line?" Carefully you tighten the drag, listening apprehensively for the staccato *pop* that would signal victory for the fish.

Getting Hooked

Your eyes are riveted on the spot in the flat sea out beyond the surf where the taut line slants down into the water. The surface around the line suddenly bulges, then erupts in a shower of spray. Striped bass don't usually jump. But for a few seconds this one hangs acrobatically in the air before splashing back into the water. You wonder if you and the fish are still connected—whether you're both still linked, physically and yes, mentally.

The answer comes quickly. An angry yank almost rips the rod from your grasp. You can feel the fish's rage. It, too, probably thought for those few instants while flying through the air that it was free.

At least you've glimpsed your prize—wide black stripes imprinted on a field of shiny silver scales. Old Linesides, as the species is nicknamed. The leap, however, seems to have strengthened the bass's resolve. The rod butt is now digging painfully into your groin, your left hand cramped from cranking the reel without gaining line.

You shout tauntingly at the fish, "By God I've got you! You're mine, you sonofabitch!"

No reason to swear at this noble beast just because he's showing the same strength and fortitude we admire in our own. But the curse words pop out.

Once again the bass is zigging and zagging wildly through the water, still very much in control of the fight. It's the wide caudal fin, rooted in a muscular tail, that enables it to change direction and accelerate so rapidly.

Few other fish are capable of making lunges, leaps, and runs like this. But then the inshore turbulence that most big fish avoid is where stripers are at home. It's their playground as well as their feeding ground. If you watch closely, sometimes you can actually see stripers frolicking in the rips and tides, and racing through the arcs of breaking waves. They may lack the sustained swiftness of sharks, tuna, and other open-ocean predators, but their bodies are flexible, built for maneuverability and the short bursts of speed needed when searching out a meal close to shore.

Without warning the line goes slack and you're now sure that you've lost your prize. "Crank fast," you say. Dripping monofilament piles up on the reel until a heavy tug tells you your fish is still there.

"Move back. Take a few steps up onto the beach," you tell yourself. "Try to turn this big boy around before he empties your reel." But the fish stubbornly refuses to turn. The reel sings and all your regained line is gone.

It's not exactly sympathy for the fish, but there comes a moment of hesitation in the battle when you momentarily wonder if this gallant fighter doesn't deserve its freedom. Its extraordinary strength and valor have already given you a year's surfcasting excitement even though the close connection with it has only existed for a matter of minutes. It's the quest, not the kill, that's the real reward in seeking to outwit a wild animal. Foxhunters thrill to the chase, not to shooting sly old Reynard once he's cornered.

These thoughts evaporate quickly. The taste of firm, mouthwatering fillets, grilled to perfection over a charcoal fire, replaces any generous, life-sparing feelings. Especially when you spot a dorsal fin slicing through the water like a knife, a signal that the big fish may finally be weakening and ready to surrender.

The trick now is to nudge it into a wave and let the force of the water wash the heavy body ashore. But it's still too game to come willingly. Instead, it bursts out of the water again, standing on its tail and shaking its head, resisting surrender.

Noticeably, though, strength is seeping from its body. Its zigs and zags are slower. And you can tell from the weaker pull on the line that it's probably too drained for another run or dive. But bass, like humans, can still generate an extraordinary exuberance when their lives are threatened.

Suddenly its surface thrashes pose other problems. Will the plug be ripped from its mouth? Will its sharp fins or tail slice the line? Even in its weakened state, you know that the odds favor the fish.

Just when you're wondering how to bring it in a heavy roller engulfs your prize and it disappears in the boiling surf, only to reemerge tumbling toward you in the shallows a few feet from shore.

Lying on its side, exhausted, the bass is even larger

than you thought. Its head is huge, the size of a dog's. The green-spotted plug that it mistook for a mackerel protrudes from its mouth like a fat cigar. You wade out into the water and slip your hand under a gasping gill and drag the spent fish up onto the beach. The fight is finally won and the big striper is yours. But do you really want to destroy this magnificent creature?

At this moment it's impossible not to think of the frailty of life, and how it can be snatched away by a whim of weather, disease, or even by diabolical human nature. Holding life-or-death power over another creature is an enormous responsibility, especially when that creature is lying helpless at your feet awaiting your decision.

Fortunately for stripers big and small, it's a decision surfcasters don't often have to make. As one outdoor writer aptly put it, "The beauty of this form of angling is that it's possible to go for long periods of time without catching a fish." Or as another surfcasting afficionado admitted, "I go to fish. Not to catch fish." For me the joy of just being alone, surrounded by nature and immersed in my own thoughts, is the real reward of surfcasting. My deepest moments of understanding come unexpectedly when I'm communing with the sea, my mind dwelling on life's many mysteries.

For this reason angling enthusiasts from the days of Izaak Walton have claimed that fishing is not simply a sport, but a religion. If this is so then surfcasting, with its own devout followers, should be recognized as an important sect.

Our morning devotions begin at daybreak in the great high-domed cathedral where the fading stars and ghostly glow of last night's moon are the candles soon to be extinguished. But before the sun's fireball rises out of the sea and sets everything ablaze, we surfcasters breathe in the new day's coolness and contemplate the good fortune that has brought us to the ocean's edge.

It is only after such a moment of reverence that our ritual begins. Almost mindlessly we check the grip of our waders on the slippery stones underfoot, open the wire bail of the spinning reel, whip the long fiberglass rod forward, and send a shiny lure affixed to the free-spooling monofilament flying off to kiss a wave.

Barely has the lure hit the water than in our mind's eye we can see the silvery flash and flying spray of a striper or blue striking the plug. It's the excitement of a strike that keeps us repeating cast after cast, although deep in our subconscious we know almost every wave is empty—devoid of fish, or at best containing one that has already feasted on so many menhaden or sand eels, its appetite is sated.

That's why the high priests of our sect who have written such how-to tomes on surfcasting as *The Salt-Water Fisherman's Bible* preach infinite patience. They realize there are many more productive ways of fishing. Trolling or jigging from a boat begets more blues, bass, and bonito—even an occasional weakfish, as the beautiful speckled sea trout are called in the Northeast. Bottom fishing off a dock or jetty can yield a mess of blacks, fluke, or flounder.

But then surfcasters are not usually out there foraging for food. Most of us are more meditative than we are meat fishermen.* We are made happy by the mere motion that sends our plug arcing through the air, and by watching expectantly as it skips back over the wavetops.

"Hit!" we murmur. "Hit!" This little word is our mind-numbing mantra. It doesn't matter that almost every cast is fruitless, completed without a hit.

Skunked is one of the most common words in the surfcaster's vocabulary. Only in recent years have I discovered that the solitude that goes with being skunked is catching—though in a different way than the catching of fish. No telling what deeply suppressed thoughts or secrets of nature will tug at my mind on those days when I'm swinging that rod back and forth without a strike.

Waves, especially, stir my imagination. On windy days with the sea slapping hard against my waders I

---

*Throughout this book my use of the term *fishermen,* rather than *fisherpersons,* is intended to include both male and female anglers.

sometimes wonder where they came from. Did they originate on the shore of some far-off continent thousands of miles of ocean away from where I'm casting? The idea of the kinetic energy in a wave traveling so far before it is dissipated by hitting my body conjures up unsettling thoughts of a personal connection with the universe that is always mystifying.

Clouds, too, catch my attention, but in a more reassuring way. With fish on the brain it's not surprising that so many clouds take on a piscine appearance. Sometimes it's a mackerel sky, resembling the mottled back of that species, which strikes me as a sign of good luck. More propitious are the long, strung-out cumulus formations in which I can distinctly make out the broad tail, eyes, nose, and underslung jaw of the striper I'm hoping to catch. Instinctively I sense that these cloud-stripers swimming across the sky are a good omen, indicating the imminence of a strike.

Surfcasting can induce a kind of coma, erasing all thoughts about nature—and everything else for that matter—while keeping the brain in neutral. In this blank state of mind, if some simple physical diversion is required, I'll engage in a little contest with myself by trying to cast farther and farther out to sea.

We surfcasters assume that as in life, the big fish are just beyond our reach, which usually is not the case. Bass, in fact, cruise so close to shore they often resist lunging at a lure until the final few yards of a retrieve. And even if they all spurn my plug, sensing it's indeed a fake fish, this doesn't stop me from going out again the next day.

Of course the thrill of marching home with a fat bluefish or gorgeous striper in hand is not to be lightly dismissed. The hunter's triumphant return is a familiar scene in history, recorded all the way back in the earliest cave paintings. But for me bringing home a fish is simply a bonus. The solitude of surfcasting is my main enjoyment—to be savored like a fine wine or a fragrant flower.

Sport or Religion?

*"God never did make a more calm, quiet,
innocent recreation than angling."*
Izaak Walton (1593–1683), *The Compleat Angler*

As some wag once said, "There's a fine line between fishing and standing on the shore like
an idiot."

Surfcasting may look this stupid and sedentary to
the uninitiated not caught in its spell, but there's a
mystique to this form of fishing that's often misunder-
stood. The idea that we landlubbing humans can occasionally lure a fish almost to the shore, then trick
this wild creature into leaping out of the boiling surf
and striking at a painted piece of wood, plastic, or

shiny metal, appears to defy all sensible expectations. Yet on occasion this miracle actually happens.

Surfcasting, to be sure, requires an unshakable faith; otherwise we'd pack up our tackle boxes and go home. Perhaps imprinted somewhere on our DNA is a vague awareness that our most distant air-breathing ancestor, the lungfish, made it all the way to the beach, even without any artificial bait coaxing it along.

River and lake fishermen similarly depend on various schemes to trick a fish into biting on fake flies, rubber worms, and other objects that aren't really food. But these inland anglers aren't constantly casting into the unknown. They begin by locating certain deep, clear pools, or murky log-infested waters beneath tree-shaded riverbanks where they know fish regularly hang out. We surfcasters, on the other hand, are almost always facing an expanse of water that stretches endlessly to the horizon, and which may or may not at any given moment contain fish. In fact, on moonless nights or foggy days we don't even have a horizon to help us maintain our physical and mental balance. This may be why freshwater fishermen think surfcasters are crazy.

They may be right. But it's also a fact that we're more devout practitioners of our particular religion. We're like confirmed churchgoers who keep casting out prayers, hoping they'll be answered with divine help if not some tangible reward. We, too, cast into a great void, expecting scant return other than the inner serenity it brings—and, on rare occasions, a fish.

There are other differences that separate us spiritually from freshwater fishermen. While both our obsessions invite a strong bond with nature, surfcasting, I maintain, can go even farther and elicit the supernatural. Staring transfixed at the washboard ripples of a calm sea, or at the rhythmic curl and crash of storm-driven waves, can trigger intuitive flashes that seem to come out of thin air. No gurgling rivers, even those rushing and eddying around massive boulders, are capable of producing such moments of mystical perception. Perhaps it's the sea's vastness and power that make it so hypnotic.

In any case, don't ask us surfcasters to explain our intuitive flashes. Like Buddhists, we realize they are too ephemeral and elusive to be captured by words. Trying to explain the sudden realizations about life that come while communing with the sea is comparable to a Zen monk trying describe "the sound of one hand clapping."

Occasionally, though, our contemplative serenity is shattered when the sea at the other end of the line suddenly explodes. Then the spiritual part of surfcasting ends, and the visceral battle between man (or woman) and fish begins.

The rod bends precariously, its fiberglass or graphite tip almost dipping into the surf for a moment as that wild thing we are connected to zigs, then zags, all the while taking drag and sending spurts of adrenaline into our bloodstream. The reel sings. Monofilament peels off the spool. With the rod butt buried in our stomach and the rod tip up, we try to budge the stubborn critter yanking on the line.

"Is it somehow anchored to the bottom?" we wonder. Stripers are known to bump their heads against the sand trying to shake a hook. But this one feels unbudgeable. "Has it wrapped the tenuously thin twenty-pound test around some underwater, barnacle-covered rock?"

Unexpectedly, it bursts out of the surf, shaking its head so hard we can hear the hooks jangle as the plug pops out of its mouth and into the air. Exhausted, but free, the big fish flops back into a wave and is gone forever.

Surfcasters know the unexpected exhilaration of having a fish on. They also know the devastating deflation of having one get off. Those two moments are the highs and lows of our religion. Even though we are programmed not to expect much success, we curse the loss of what we are certain—and later boast—would have been a record catch.

Cursing, I fear, is a part of our tradition. Understandably so, because as both sport and religion surfcasting is full of frustration. A simple backlash, for instance, can loose a burst of bad words. But that's nothing compared to the hot lava of profanity provoked by a pair of crossed lines. This results in the ridiculous situation of two surfcasters each being sure they've hooked a monster fish, only to discover in due course that they are trying to reel each other in.

The truth is, we surfcasters are of a rougher cut than our fly-casting cousins. We not only swear a lot but look a good deal grubbier, too. We wear moth-eaten sweaters and oil-stained pants hidden under our foul-weather gear, and prefer to fish unshowered and unshaven, sometimes for several days running, sub-sisting on Beer Nuts and Slim Jims.

During the fall striper run members of our sect, if they sleep at all, can be found catnapping in beach buggies and vans, often with their waders still on. But then we just don't fathom those tweedy trout fisher-men who wield dainty four-ounce rods and fish with flies so small you can barely see them.

For surfcasters, though, there is nothing so awe in-spiring as thundering waves crashing down around our knees, followed by the death rattle of stones be-ing sucked back into the surf. On the stormiest days the spiritual high is so overpowering we have been known to shout with joy or emit a primal scream, caus-ing members of our surfcasting sect to be mistaken for hymn-shouting Pentacostals.

There is, however, one similarity between freshwa-ter fly fishermen and surfcasters. Just as they each have a favorite river, we each have our favorite seashore. Some of us prefer the Florida Keys, or the Outer

Banks of North Carolina. Others find Cape Cod, Martha's Vineyard, or Nantucket more to their liking. Then there's Cuttyhunk, a lesser-known Massachusetts island where striper fanatics from New York City built an exclusive surfcasting club more than one hundred years ago.

Striper fishing is also popular in San Francisco Bay and other Pacific coast waters. In fact, one of the most interesting experiments in fish management involved the seeding of stripers on the West Coast back in 1879. Details are fuzzy, but it is known that a number of small bass were seined from the Navesink River in New Jersey and transported by train across the continent in milk cans.

The water had to be changed frequently and agitated constantly. When the train crossed the Mississippi, a few of the stripers were tossed into the river— "just for luck," according to the skimpy written record of this interocean transfer. Only 435 fish survived the trip. But twenty years later the annual Pacific commercial catch of stripers reached 1,234,000 pounds, and remarkably from waters where this species had never existed before. In 1935 the commercial netting of stripers was banned on the west coast. Considered gamefish ever since, they now abound from San Diego northward to the Columbia River in Washington.

As a New Englander and ardent surfcaster, my favorite place is the eleven-square-mile, pork-chop-shaped outcropping in the Atlantic Ocean called Block

Island. It sits some twelve miles out to sea, midway between Montauk Point on the eastern tip of Long Island and Point Judith at the mouth of Rhode Island's Narragansett Bay.

What makes this speck of land (actually, a third bigger than the embattled World War II Pacific island of Iwo Jima) such a magnet for surfcasters is its variety of fishing environments, each with it own distinctive beauty. At Southeast Light, beneath the two-hundred-foot-high bluffs where Block's indigenous Manissean Indians once sent the invading Mohegans from Montauk hurtling to their deaths, there are giant boulders to cast from. Just three miles away at Black Rock, on the island's wide southern end, are steep, pebbly beaches with roaring surf; at the island's pointed northern tip, plumes of white spray shoot skyward above a two-mile-long sandbar separating the Atlantic Ocean from Rhode Island Sound. A monster blue or bass, or even a weakfish, can sometimes be pulled from the froth created by the colliding waves of these two bodies of water. Casting into this maelstrom, however, can be hazardous—as one hapless fisherman found when his waders filled with water and he was swept off the sandbar and drowned.

There are many less dangerous yet still challenging spots. On Block's western side, facing the faint, low-lying silhouette of New York's Fishers Island and the out-of-sight Connecticut coast directly behind it, are numerous rocky promontories and sandy coves best reachable by four-wheel-drive jeeps and beach buggies. During the fall striper run it's not unusual to see surfcasters standing almost shoulder to shoulder and hip to hip in the shallow waves of Southwest Point, or in the rocky, roiled waters of a cove with the unlikely name of Pots and Kettles, at the northeast end of the island.

Then there's the Cut, the narrow, six-hundred-foot-long channel leading into Great Salt Pond where the tide runs like a fast-flowing river. Standing on its steep sandy bank on an early-summer morning or evening you can occasionally see the stripes on little schoolies swimming by just a few feet from shore. And by late August bullet-fast bonito and false albacore—members of the tuna family—are streaking in out of the Cut chasing sand eels. This is the favorite spot of the island's fast-growing crop of saltwater fly fishermen—many of whom, like nonpracticing Catholics, are "fallen-away" plug casters.

Besides its natural beauty, Block Island is rich in lore and legend, providing fishermen with plenty of food for thought in the absence of fish. Bloody battles between white traders and Indians, and a profusion of pirates—including Captain Kidd, who buried treasure here that has never been found—are all part of its turbulent past.

A hundred years ago visiting sailors were susceptible to "falling in love with the local lassies"—or so one of the sailors wrote—despite the "disagreeable odor imparted to their dresses or persons from the burning of tug," as the native peat was called. "This being virtually the islanders only fuel," added the sailor, "they can be as readily distinguished by the nose as by the eye, or by the ear, for that matter, because of their peculiar nasal twang."

During Prohibition the island became a secret entry point for rumrunners (Sarsaparilla Boys, as they were called on Block), bringing shiploads of bootlegged booze from Canada and the Caribbean into the United States. Some islanders claim that they really weren't smuggling it into the country, because Block Island had declared its neutrality and seceded from the United States during the War of 1812 and never officially rejoined the Union. These same islanders therefore lightheartedly contend that they and the other 850 year-round residents should not be paying federal taxes, and should be represented in Washington by an ambassador instead of a congressman.

Washingtonians, on the other hand, consider Block an ideal place to escape the capital's summer heat. Bermuda of the North, they call it. During one particularly sweltering summer, Chief Justice (and former president) William Howard Taft moved the entire Supreme Court into the island's Ocean View Hotel, which burned to the ground in 1966. There is no record of whether or not the "nine old men" took time off from their serious business to wet a line.

Some of our most illustrious presidents also came

to cool off, and a couple even tried their hand at surf-casting. Ulysses S. Grant was the first commander in chief to enjoy the island's summer breezes, though only briefly when he stopped in for lunch and a quick look at the newly erected Southeast Light in 1875. Franklin Roosevelt, however, twice tested his fishing skills at Block, in 1935 and 1937, and according to local headlines with no luck either time. Dwight Eisenhower proved more successful, casting for bonito off a boat at the entrance to Great Salt Pond.

But Ike, a veteran fly caster, arrived with the wrong gear and had to borrow a couple of Tony Accetta lures from a local lad, whose tackle box, incidentally, the president never returned. Bill Clinton dropped by in a helicopter for a quick look at the island and a Ben & Jerry's ice-cream cone in 1997 on his way to Martha's Vineyard. Block has no golf course; otherwise this nonfishing president might have stayed longer.

More than a magnet for presidents, Block Island has drawn some 350 luckless vessels of various sizes to its dangerous shoals. Half of all the shipwrecks in the Northeast have occurred in these rock-infested and frequently fog-shrouded waters. But given the island's location smack in the middle of the busy sea-lanes emanating from New York, Providence, and Boston, that's hardly surprising.

Block has even benefited from a few of these wrecks. When the 180-foot schooner *Jacob S. Winslow* struck Black Rock during a gale in 1914 and quickly broke up, her cargo of hard pine was used to build the local power company's plant. The mast from the steam trawler *Petrel,* wrecked in 1930, was converted into a flagpole for the island's new school. And that same year the *Edward Luckenbach* went aground in a heavy fog and had to jettison her cargo: thousands of tons of canned food, which helped feed islanders forced to subsist mainly on fish during the Great Depression. But every evening meal provided by the *Luckenbach* was a potluck supper, because the labels had washed off the cans. Today, an illustrated map depicting the name and date of all 350 ships that have sunk at Block is a favorite souvenir for tourists.

Another shipwreck souvenir, though pursued only by daring deep-sea divers, is pieces of fancy dinnerware raised from the Italian luxury liner *Andrea Doria.* Rammed in a thick fog by the Swedish ship *Stockholm* during the summer of 1956, she sank in two hundred feet of water, ten miles northeast of the island.

So you see, Block's colorful past offers a lot to think about when one wearies of casting and decides to sit on the beach in slack water and wait for the tide to change. For those interested in the island's history, there are numerous published accounts available at three local bookstores. Surprisingly, there is one more bookstore than there are tackle shops on the island.

But then, during its long, desolate winters, a lot more reading (and drinking) than fishing is done by the year-round residents. That's probably been true ever since the first European settlers landed here in 1661.

For me, at least, knowing a bit about Block's rugged history makes it a more interesting place to surfcast. The first written description of the island, I discovered, appeared in 1524 in the ship's log of Florentine explorer Giovanni da Verrazano. He named it Claudia in honor of the mother of his royal patron, King Francis I of France.

Verrazano's log also noted numerous fires burning along the shore, an account corroborated later by historians, who estimate that some three thousand Indians inhabited the island at that time. The Indians called their home Manisses, meaning "Isle of the Little God." Today, while casting out into the roaring surf, it's hard to imagine anybody in a flimsy birch-bark canoe negotiating the rough stretch of ocean between Block and the mainland, as these Native Americans must have done.

However they managed to get here, the Indians' name for the place was much more descriptive than the current one. *Block* to me sounds like some gray slab of concrete sticking up out of the ocean, rather than the sliver of land fringed with pristine sand beaches and covered with goldenrod and greenery as it appears today from one of the small commuter planes that shuttle back and forth to the mainland. But for some inexplicable reason it was the name of the Dutch trader and navigator Adriaen Block, who landed in 1614, that stuck. His original ship and cargo of furs had burned in New York Harbor, and he arrived aboard a new sixteen-ton vessel christened the *Unrest*. As history was soon to prove, that would have been a more appropriate name for the island.

Serious unrest began on Block in 1636 when the Indians murdered a white trader from Boston. In reprisal, ninety British soldiers dispatched by the governor of the Massachusetts Bay Colony waded ashore clad in armor, with their muskets held high over the surf, and stove in the Indians' canoes, burned their wigwams and cornfields, and then slaughtered or maimed a sizable portion of the male population. The rough stone markers where the Indians buried their dead have now become a sight-seeing attraction for visiting anglers, especially on hot windless days when the fishing off the beach is just as dead as those Indians.

It's pretty clear from the piles of old clam and oyster shells found around the island, along with stone axes and flint arrowheads, that the local tribe savored seafood as much as we do today. The island's taxi drivers, who double as tour guides, claim the Indians were such seafood lovers that they left a clay bowl full of stewed bluefish or striped bass beside each grave to sustain the deceased while he was in transit to the "happy hunting (and fishing) grounds" of his next life.

Sometimes after making one unproductive cast after another with my modern fishing gear, I marvel at how the primitively equipped Indians snagged blues and stripers with only a clam or sea worm impaled on a hand-carved bone hook. Of course, in their day there were no commercial fishing fleets constantly circling the island, scooping up whole schools of blues, bass, or mackerel on each sweep. Sadly, we're now left to cast for the strays that elude the outstretched nets of these "draggers."

What makes Block particularly attractive today to surfcasters, who ferry or fly in from all over the East, is the proximity of one good fishing location to another. If conditions at one point, cove, or beach don't seem right, it's just a quick drive or a short hike to another. And if you've been skunked and happen to be crossing the island after sunup, a brief stop at Bethany's Airport Diner for a short stack and a warming cup of coffee can be mighty restorative.

Customers clad in dripping waders are always welcome. Waders, in fact, appear to be part of Bethany's dress code. But when you're sitting at the counter piled high with muffins and Danish and enjoying the aroma of freshly brewed coffee, the early-morning banter can suddenly make you sick to your stomach. Especially if you've been skunked and some local redneck user of live eels for bait is bragging about the forty-five-pound striper he hauled in an hour earlier—and just a short cast down the beach from where you were trying one plug after another without a strike. But don't doubt his word. Indeed, I once challenged the veracity of one of these live-eel bait slingers, only to have him lug the lunker, still opening and closing its enormous gills, right into Bethany's. "Hit like a blacksmith striking an anvil," he announced to all the breakfasters gathered there.

What in the world, I wondered, did Izaak Walton mean when he wrote that "God never did make a more calm, quiet, innocent recreation than angling?" God obviously never tried casting a line into Block Island's boiling surf. And if He did, I'm certain He would have used an artificial lure so as to spare the life of an eel.

3

Lures to Lure
the Fisherman

"Fish, not with this melancholy bait."
William Shakespeare (1564–1616), *The Merchant of Venice*

The first settlers in New England were known to
have gone surfcasting for striped bass as early
as 1634. But they didn't consider it a sport. Nor
did they care about its uplifting spiritual effect. For
them surfcasting was strictly a matter of gastronomics.
Wrote an appreciative angler named William Wood:

> The basse is one of the best fishes in the countrye,
> and although men are soon wearied with other fish,

yet they are never with the basse. It is a delicate, fine, fat fish having a bone in its head which contains a saucer full of marrow, sweet and good, pleasant to the pallat, and wholesome to the stomach.

It could also be argued that the bait used by Wood and his fellow surfcasters was even more pleasant to the palate than the fish it enticed. In colonial days a succulent piece of lobster meat was attached to a bare hook, and a two-pound hunk of lead tied to the end of a heavy line. The angler then twirled the weighted line lasso-style above his head before flinging it out into the sea. But the lead drail had to be scraped with a knife after every few casts so it would stay bright and attract fish. Any stripers hauled in by this crude procedure were promptly clubbed to death on the beach.

This so-called heave-and-haul method of surfcasting was gradually improved over the years. Longer heaves, it was found, could be made if the line was first coiled in a basket suspended from the surfcaster's neck by a leather thong. Various other natural baits, including eels, mossbunker, and squid, gradually replaced the choice chunks of lobster.

Rod-and-reel surfcasting didn't begin until after the Civil War. Originally a rich man's sport in Massachusetts and Rhode Island, this more sophisticated form of fishing was mostly confined to striped bass clubs on Cuttyhunk, Martha's Vineyard, Pasque Island, Squibnocket, West Island, and Cohasset Narrows. Wealthy

Bostonians and New Yorkers happily paid a thousand-dollar initiation fee to join one of these exclusive groups, where they could surfcast in complete comfort. A roost of carrier pigeons at each club kept the anglers in contact with their offices.

Attached to the clubhouses were long piers, or "fishing stands," extending up to one hundred feet out into the water. Chairs were provided so the anglers, who dressed in ties and jackets, could sit down between casts. Making the sport cushier still was the "chummer" or "gillie" assigned to each fisherman. His job was to fillet the baitfish, place it on the hook, and then toss the head, tail, and entrails into the water to create an oily slick that would bring the stripers within casting distance. Blues were considered trash fish, and were either released or cut up for chum.

When a bass was hooked, all the angler had to do was play it close enough to the fishing stand for the gillie to gaff. The day of fishing was capped with an elegant silver-service supper in the clubhouse. Mainly a social event for the elite, surfcasting in those days was far from evolving into today's national obsession with its millions of faithful adherents.

Casting gear was also expensive. Rods were made either of greenheart, a tropical South American wood, Calcutta cane, or Bombay bamboo. "Male" bamboo, which has an almost solid center and a short space between nodes, was considered superior to the "female" bamboo, which is almost hollow and has a larger space between nodes. I hasten to mention that this sexist nomenclature originated with British bamboo traders in India and not with the author of this book.

The reels back then were oversized versions of the handmade brass or silver freshwater models turned out by watchmakers. Jeweled bushings reduced the friction so the braided silk or twisted Irish linen line could be cast farther and more smoothly. However, the line had to be washed and dried after every outing. Nobody even dreamed of a single synthetic filament that would be almost invisible in water, or of a spinning reel that would allow the line to peel, with great speed, off a stationary spool.

Although better equipment was being developed, little was known about the habits of the striped bass. Finally, in the early 1900s, just when marine biologists were becoming interested in stripers, the species suddenly and unaccountably almost vanished from the New England coast. The colorful old clubs disappeared, and so did the fishermen. Only the defunct Cuttyhunk clubhouse still stands, a souvenir of surfcasting's more elegant past.

Just as mysteriously as the stripers left, they suddenly reappeared in great numbers in 1936. By then manufacturers were mass-producing rods and reels at reasonable prices. Also, automobiles made easily accessible what had previously been considered remote beaches up and down the East Coast.

Further popularizing all saltwater gamefishing was

a new crop of adventure writers including Zane Grey and Ernest Hemingway, both of whom touted the man-versus-fish contest as a macho sport. By the end of World War II surfcasting had become a booming business. Several technological discoveries made during the war also spilled over into surfcasting—neoprene waders, fiberglass rods, molded plastic plugs, and the fixed-spool spinning reel became popular. A wave of returning veterans converted old army jeeps into beach buggies and fished constantly to forget their days in combat.

The convenience and low cost of casting from the shore, compared to trolling from a boat, added still more followers to the cult. As anyone who's ever owned a boat knows, it's both time consuming and expensive. That old saw about the happiest day in a man's life being the day he bought a boat, and the second happiest being the day he sold it, is true.

Trolling takes its toll in other ways as well, since it's often an excuse for a bunch of guys to go on a beer-drinking toot. Sunburn and a six-pack are a killer combination. By the time the bachelor party of trollers returns to port and hoses down the boat, many hours, if not they themselves, are shot.

Surfcasting, on the other hand, offers healthy exercise, which can be squeezed in before or after work or even at night, when it's usually most productive.

There is also the added challenge of catching fish that fight harder in close to shore. Both stripers and blues make longer, more desperate runs as the water gets shallower. Stripers, especially, will swim, leap, roll, and lunge with an amount of pure energy that surpasses almost anything in the sea. When they race through the arc of a breaking wave, they use the power in their broad tails to master this wild water that no other fish dares to navigate.

Meanwhile, the fisherman must stand firm amid those same crashing waves, playing his wily prey. If he's smart he'll get the surf to work for him, pumping the fish shoreward on the crest of each wave, and then letting it slip back in the undertow. Eventually a wave will wash the exhausted bass or blue high and dry on the shore. But the odds are with the fish, so when a big bass or blue is finally beached, it's quite a victory.

Surfcasting, in my opinion, can lift the human spirit like no other solo activity. It provides a lot of uninterrupted time to think, or to turn off the brain and absorb nature's offerings—fiery sunrises and sunsets, silvery moonlight, cottony clouds, booming surf, and the cold, stinging salt spray that blows off the wavetops. The wind and sea together hum a wild harmony that vibrates like nothing else in my veins.

Of course, this harmonizing effect improves with a fish on the line. But whether a fish ultimately strikes or not depends partly on the tide, wind direction, time of day or night, and, to a great extent, what the surfcaster tosses in its direction. That's why a trip to the tackle shop is such a turn-on.

On Block Island, happily, there are two such places to hook us surfcasters: Oceans and Ponds, an Orvis franchise owned by retired New York City investment banker Bruce Johnson, and Twin Maples, where proprietor Matthew "Mac" Swienton is a magician at dissecting and reassembling surfcasting equipment. But without his pacemaker this octogenarian's heart would not run smoothly, and neither would most of the salt-encrusted spinning reels on the island.

It's impossible to spurn the wall displays at these two tackle shops. The sight of so many shiny, chromed Kastmasters, Krocodiles, and Hopkinses—and even more tantalizing, all the brightly painted plugs—stirs my yearning to go surfcasting the same way the mouth-watering buffet at the island's 1661 Inn stimulates my appetite for brunch after a long morning of fishing. But which lure will make a blue, striper, bonito, or weakfish salivate? That's the crucial question.

Although fish do have tongues and taste buds that help them decide whether to swallow or spit out what's in their mouths, they are often hooked before they can make that decision. So I keep trying to pretend I'm a fish and pick the size, color, and shape of lure that looks most appetizing. I tend to shun "tins," as the spoons, Swedish Pimples, diamond jigs, and other metal lures are called, in favor of plugs.

Basically, there are only two types of plugs—poppers

that skip along the surface and swimmers that travel deep. The problem is, both kinds come in infinite sizes and shapes. Some are stubby and hollow nosed, others long and needle nosed. Their wiggle in the water, however, depends on whether they are made of a solid piece of wood or plastic, or are jointed in the middle to swim more irregularly. There is also a full rainbow of colors to choose from.

One of the most frequent questions asked by anglers is, "Are fish color-blind?" The answer is no. A marine biologist's experiment with a school of snapper blues living under a dock revealed that they would devour tasty red pellets but avoid yellow ones that didn't taste good. Freshwater fish are not color-blind either. Largemouth bass, it was discovered, have a natural preference for red, but they can be trained in controlled environments to associate one color with food and another color with something unpleasant, such as an electric shock. Hatchery trout also show an affinity for red.

My own experience indicates that bluefish prefer silver surface plugs, while stripers go for dark, mottled green surface plugs or deep swimmers that resemble mackerel. I've also found wooden plugs, which can be reeled in more slowly because they won't sink, to outperform those made of plastic.

But the choice of lures doesn't end there. Some plugs come festooned with treble hooks, others with a less lethal barbless single hook affixed to its rear end for casting where it's weedy. Some have tufted tails or googoo eyes, designed, I suppose, to make them look sexier, or at least to give them more angler appeal. Of course that's the dilemma: What catches the fisherman's eye may not catch fish.

Producing a plug that has instant angler appeal is the goal of all lure manufacturers. Like women's fashions, the popularity of plug styles changes from season to season and from one location to another. But that's hardly surprising, given the premise that surfcasting begins with the lure, a fact often obscured by techno-mad tackle manufacturers that trumpet the introduction of each new rod, reel, or other gadget in outdoor magazines.

But the plug is prior. It's the surfcasting equivalent of "where the rubber meets the road" or, more precisely, where the tackle meets the fish. For this reason, never mind how many dozens of lures you have at home. It's almost impossible to escape from a well-stocked tackle shop without buying another.

One of the most insidious things about these stores is the photo displays of fishermen posing with their catches, which are usually placed right beside the cash register. The strategic location of these snapshots, I've come to realize, is to divert attention from the large sums of money being handed over for a couple of brightly colored pieces of wood, plastic, or metal, which surely can't cost much to make.

The snapshots usually show: 1) A smiling ten-year-old lad hefting a striper that just about outweighs him;

2) a string of humongous blues suspended tail-down from a clothesline; 3) a freshly caught weakfish laid out on the sand before its brilliant colors have begun to fade. The photographs are always undated, so it's impossible to tell if these great catches occurred yesterday or yesteryear when the aforementioned gamefish were more abundant.

Another entrapment trick of tackle shops is their offering of an almost limitless choice of accessories. A simple leader, for instance, can be made of either wire or monofilament, and with an almost infinite variety of swiveled or unswiveled snaps that permit rapid plug changes. There are standard snaps, interlock snaps, McMahon snaps (shaped like ice tongs), and several other kinds. I happen to prefer casting without a leader or snap, and with my line tied directly to the plug, even though that gives the fish a better chance of chewing through the thin monofilament or slicing it with a fin.

Stripers or weakfish especially can be so picky, I worry that any extra hardware attached to a plug will convince even the hungriest that he's chasing an ersatz minnow. The Atom Company, which makes Striper Swipers and other popular lures, warns customers in the literature that comes with its plugs that fish today are warier than they used to be. "With so much catch-and-release fishing," Atom states, "we believe fish can encode the danger of lures into their genes." Sounds like a fish story, doesn't it?

There are, nevertheless, certain precautions to take.

When tying on a plug, make sure there's no suntan lotion or bug spray on your fingers. Fish can indeed smell. They have sensitive olfactory nerves connected to their nostrils, or "nares," to be ichthyologically correct. In fact, they are endowed with two pairs of nares, all the better to smell with.

When no single lure seems to entice a striper, a so-called teaser or dropper, consisting of a fly or rubber sand eel, can be tied on the line so that it skips through the water four or five inches ahead of the plug. The theory is that a striper will be doubly tempted. Ichthyologists attribute the added attraction of a teaser to what they claim is the "competitive feeding response" ingrained in the fish's brain. In other words, they contend a fish is more attracted to a prey that is being chased. It's been my experience that a striper will most often go for the teaser first, probably figuring it can then turn around and gobble up the attacker. But things don't always work that way.

One windless dawn I was casting into the tidal flow pouring through the Cut. The water's glassy surface was etched with the swirls of feeding stripers. Schoolies for sure, they were in so close to shore that I could occasionally glimpse their stripes lit by the sun's first rays.

These young bass were driving me crazy. Cast after cast I watched dorsal fins slicing through the water behind my silver popper, but not one damn fish made a lunge for the lure. I was about to give up and go get some breakfast when the plug dipped below the surface and disappeared.

"Okay, you finicky bastard," I shouted. "I finally fooled you."

A moment later the surface erupted and the fish flew out of the water. It wasn't a small striper but an enormous blue.

For no particular reason, I had opted that morning for a light, eight-foot rod with four-pound-test line. Instantly, the thin tip curled down into the water. In fact the whole flimsy rod almost flipped into the water.

With such delicate monofilament and no leader, I expected the line to be quickly sliced by the blue's sharp teeth or a swipe of its tail.

I loosened the drag and let the fish run for deep water in the middle of the channel. Luckily it was too early for the usual morning parade of boats coming in and out of the harbor.

After every hard tug I gave the fish more line, until I spotted it splashing in the shallows near the opposite side of the Cut.

"We'll just have to see who gets tired first," I thought. The sun's red ball was already poking up over the trees and a couple of other surfcasters had now arrived, humorously enjoying my plight as I kept trying to gain a little line without horsing the heavy fish. You couldn't call it a fight, because I was pretty much letting this big blue have its way.

"Come to me, baby," I yelled. And as if suddenly responding to my cajoling, the fish turned and started swimming toward where my two feet were planted in the sand. "Keep coming," I hollered, much to the amusement of the two men who, rods in hand, were now standing beside me, kibbitzing.

I kept reeling in slack as the fish continued swimming in my direction. Then suddenly finding itself in shallow water, it began to thrash furiously. Too late. I waded in, grabbed a gill, and dragged the writhing creature up on the sand.

The three-foot-long blue looked deformed. A large lump protruded from the side of its stomach, as if it were pregnant and about to give birth. When I slit open its belly, a twelve-inch striper popped out with hardly a tooth mark on it. The young bass must have been chasing my lure when the blue caught sight of them both and swallowed the bass whole, before greedily grabbing the lure it had been chasing. Proof positive, I thought, of the ichthyologists' competitive feeding response theory. But in this case the blue went for the larger, more appetizing attacker first.

Bluefish, or choppers as they're sometimes called, are more often disgustingly undiscriminating about their diet, though they're not as bad as cod— which swim with their mouths open, swallowing whatever fits into their gaping maws. Blues are a savage bunch, out to bite, mangle, or swallow whole every smaller fish in their path, including their own young. The carnage they create could give any self-respecting shark an inferiority complex.

One of the blue's favorite foods is the silverside, a brilliant slender dart that measures about three inches long. During summer, most of the gluttonous bluefish caught in the Northeast will be found to have bellies crammed full of these baitfish.

John Hersey, in his wonderful book *Blues,* describes the terrible dent made in the food chain by a single bluefish. He claims it takes some fifty pounds of silversides to produce one five-pound blue. At the same time, it takes five hundred pounds of plankton, composed of millions of single-celled diatoms, to produce the silversides. Finally, at the bottom of the food chain, five thousand pounds of microscopic sea plants are required to produce the tiny plankton animals.

Blues don't commit their wholesale butchery just for nourishment. Sometimes as soon as their stomachs are bulging, they vomit up the contents and start over. Blues, in fact, are so voracious they're known to consume seven or eight times their weight in a day.

Their gluttonous feeding habits have been studied in a thirty-two-thousand-gallon tank at the Sandy Hook, New Jersey, Marine Laboratory. Spotting a prey, a hungry blue was seen bursting ahead, reaching a speed of fifteen knots with its eyes fixed forward, mouth wide open, and gill plates flared. If the prey was too long to swallow in one gulp, it would be bitten in half, or if too thick, chewed up as the blue shook its head from side to side. Even with its stomach bulging after feeding on small prey, a blue would attack a larger prey with the same gusto as if it hadn't already eaten. According to the scientists at Sandy Hook, the sight of the larger prey signaled the blue's brain that here was something so appetizing it shouldn't be passed up.

Blues' murderous attacks haven't always been confined to the finny world. During World War II, huge thirty-pound Mediterranean members of this species were reported to have attacked American fliers who bailed out over the North African coast. Having personally witnessed wolf packs of hungry blues chasing vast schools of panic-stricken menhaden clear up onto the beach, I find this report entirely believable.

Deliberating over the perfect plug to entice a bluefish is a waste of time. Success is mainly a matter of casting far enough to reach a school. The schools are usually easy to spot: Just watch for flocks of diving gulls and terns feasting on the leftovers chopped up by the needle-sharp teeth of these fish when they are in one of their collective feeding frenzies.

It doesn't seem to matter how many lures a surfcaster accumulates, there's always one favorite in every tackle box. Look for the plug with the peeling paint and most teeth marks. My preference is for surface plugs. I want to seduce some prize into surfacing so I can see it strike, not just feel it hit. The visual part adds to the excitement. Then even if the fish misses, which is often the case, at least I've had the thrill of watching it whack at this thing I've been casting count- less times with no takers. When using a spoon or deep- swimming plug there's no telling if a fish is even in the vicinity until it actually strikes.

There are plenty of live-bait slingers and chunkers (users of cut bait) who shun artificial lures entirely. But because of my inherent revulsion to bait, they strike me as throwbacks to the dawn of fishing, when Stone Age men tossed a piece of meat on a wooden gorge out into the ocean. Using the same tactic today, bait slingers impale their weighted hooks with wriggling eels or cut-up chunks of mackerel, menhaden, or squid before hurling the whole slimy mess out into the surf.

I've stooped to using live menhaden, but only once, and while fishing from a boat. I was anchored just a few feet from shore, and decided to drive crazy any stripers that happened to be lurking in the rocks below by placing three trolling rods in the boat's stern rod holders, each rigged with a live menhaden. I loos- ened the drag on the reels so that if a big bass came along, it could gulp down the baitfish and take off on a good run before the hook caught in the lining of its stomach. I then rigged a casting rod with a fourth menhaden and dangled it off the bow. I was watching this foot-long baitfish swimming happily to and fro, delighted (I assumed) to be out of the boat's live well and back in the sea, when a monster bass lumbered out from under the boat and grabbed it. At that same moment I heard all three reels in the stern start to sing.

Desperately hanging on to the casting rod with its pulsating tip curled down into the water, I worked my way aft toward the three other rods, hoping to tighten the drags before their reels ran out of line. But before I could reach them the four lines became hopelessly tangled. For a second I was tempted to jump overboard and grab one of the thrashing stripers by the tail and toss it into the boat. Then as I watched in disbelief, one after another of the four bass broke free. Served me right, I decided, for using live bait.

Rigging a live eel, however, is a lot more unsavory than slipping a hook through a menhaden's back. Read Gary Caputi's description in *Fishing for Striped Bass* of how to bait a slithering live eel by running the hook up through its chin and out its eye socket, and you won't have much of a stomach for this kind of fishing. Even less appealing are his instructions for running a long-shank hook out a squirming eel's anal vent.

Bait slingers, in any case, are a sedentary bunch who miss out on all the exercise and excitement of casting from a beach. Once his firmly hooked eel or mackerel chunk has sunk to the bottom, watch and you'll often see one stick his rod in a sand spike, plop down in a folding chair, and pop open a beer to relieve the boredom that's sure to follow. These bait slingers are easy to identify. They wear KISS MY BASS T-shirts, and cowboy boots instead of waders. Of course, if a bass hits they'll leap into action, provided they haven't fallen asleep.

There is a middle way between surfcasting with live bait and artificial lures. One of the surest striped bass killers is the so-called rigged eel. But the unpleasant advance preparation involves killing the eel and replacing its innards with a plain cedar plug, or taking an eel skin and wiring it to a lead head.

Although all live-bait fishermen swear by eels, the truth is that a hungry striped bass, like a bluefish, will attack and eat anything that swims, creeps, or crawls in salt water. That's why stripers are called the vacuum cleaners of the sea. Once to my surprise I cut open the belly of a striper and found a rock with tendrils of seaweed attached to it.

According to Erwin A. Bauer, author of *The Salt-Water Fisherman's Bible,* the live-bait versus artificial-lure debate all depends on whether a striper is mad, hungry, or just curious. An artificial lure, Bauer claims, will incite the fish to strike if it's angry. If it's feeding, live bait works best. But if it's just curious, there's no telling what will attract it. Everything from seagull feathers to cigarette lighters has been found inside the stomachs of stripers.

Casting for
Fresh Ideas

*"Yes, as everyone knows meditation
and water are wedded forever."*
Herman Melville (1819–91), *Moby Dick*

Melville and many other writers of sea stories have described how conducive the ocean is to the probing of man's innermost thoughts. We surfcasters have likewise discovered for ourselves that the ocean's sounds, motion, and color can massage the mind into releasing thoughts and ideas buried in its deepest recesses. That's why the catching of a fish is merely one of the rewards obtained from taking rod and reel in hand and trodding the sand of a deserted beach.

It's more true than ever today when our eyes, ears, and brains are being bombarded by faxes, e-mail, voice mail, junk mail, cellular phones, and of course the ubiquitous TV, fed by round-the-clock satellited news transmissions from Baghdad, Belgrade, Beijing, and, from the heart of Africa, Ouagadougou. Surfing the Internet, I maintain, is not nearly as good for the soul as casting into the surf. But wouldn't you know it, software has been devised so fishing fanatics can now cast on their computer screens for cyberstripers.

Neophyte surfcasters don't understand the importance of the quest—how tramping a deserted beach, all the while trying to coax an occasional fish out of the thundering waves, can nurture the soul and relax the mind into revealing its deepest secrets. These obscure benefits, I believe, can only be absorbed intuitively over time. They can't be taught.

On the other hand, it's easy enough to teach beginners the rudimentary mechanics of surfcasting—the different ways of swinging a rod, or retrieving a lure to make it look alive, or playing a fish to keep it from breaking off, or finally, at the end of a hard fight, using the action of the waves to help land the exhausted animal.

Maybe it's beginner's luck, but both stripers and blues have proved surprisingly cooperative whenever I've been asked to give a lesson. I've rarely been skunked on those occasions, which prompted my wife to once remark that maybe I ought to quit wasting my time fishing and become a guide.

Look at what happened with my ten-year-old nephew. His previous fishing experience was limited to casting into a placid little pond for smallmouth bass. So he was rightly skeptical about his chances of pulling a bass ten or twenty times this size out of the unruly surf.

I was standing behind him, holding on to his two spindly arms as he completed his first practice cast, when a twenty-five-pound striper grabbed the plug and started tearing off line. Clinging to the startled boy to keep him from being dragged deeper into the surf, I fought that fish with him for twenty minutes. Only when the striper was more spent than my nephew did I let go of the boy so he could feel the thrill of landing the fish by himself.

Another time on a beach picnic, the hamburgers and hot dogs were already sizzling over a hot driftwood fire when I suggested to one of the women present that she try her hand at surfcasting. "You might just add a tasty item to our dinner menu," I teased.

"But I've never done it," she protested.

"One demonstration cast," I said. "That's all you need."

Bang! My plug had barely hit the water when a giant blue leapt out of a wave and smashed at it. But the sucker missed, so I gave the rod a yank. The plug took a short skip and the blue struck again, this time clamping its sharp teeth on the wood, the hooks digging into its mouth. Without a word of warning I thrust the violently vibrating rod into the woman's hands.

Looking back on the incident, I guess I expected her to flee, terror stricken. Instead, she began reeling furiously. With jutted jaw and furrowed brow, she was determined to make quick work of that fish. Obviously, she didn't consider this a sport, or a moment of excitement to be savored. As a mother and the good provider she had probably always been, her single concern was supplementing the fare of our picnic with a succulent first course. Ten minutes later a couple of fat bluefish fillets were sizzling on the grate beside the burgers.

Beginner's luck like this—particularly when the tangible results are instantly appreciated—doesn't help anyone understand what surfcasting can do for the soul. It took me many a fishless morning, and endless evenings of being skunked, for this awakening to occur. Only slowly did I come to realize that for me, at least, it wasn't the fish so much as the solitude and chance for reflection that was the most fulfilling aspect of this activity.

To unburden the mind as well as the body during surfcasting forays, it helps to travel light. One rod and reel, a few lures, and a knife is all I bring with me. No pliers, no whetstone, no rod belt, no "fish slugger" (also known as a "priest," because it administers the last rites to the fish), no bug spray, no food, no folding chair—not even waders if the water's warm. As far as beach buggies go, they're as bad as using helicopters to hunt wolves.

The modern business management acronym KISS (Keep It Simple, Stupid) applies to surfcasting as well. Part of the sport's calming effect on the mind comes from the simple repetitive action of flinging out a plug and reeling it in. The motions become so automatic and attention-free that the brain can then delve into its subconscious and produce what parapsychologists call an altered state or sixth sense. This sixth sense, they claim, enables us humans to view things our eyes can't see.

Eastern mystics have insisted for centuries that getting into such an altered state of mind is a prerequisite for understanding the deeper meanings of life. In *Zen in the Art of Archery*, German philosopher Eugen Herrigel, who studied in Japan, explains how the concentration and, most particularly, the "self-forgetfulness" involved in shooting a bow and arrow can produce this liberating mental effect. He claims that the brain-freeing act of focusing on a target while drawing back the bowstring, and then releasing it, allows the mind to turn inward and "let go of its limited consciousness in favor of a vastly expanded one."

A rod and reel can do the same thing. The rote process of casting out and retrieving a plug satisfies the four basic requirements described by Eastern mystics for relaxing the mind and expanding consciousness.

First of all, surfcasting is carried out in a peaceful environment. It matters not that the ocean itself can be thunderous, or that the honking of geese or plaintive cry of gulls wheeling overhead adds to the seaside cacophany. There are no honking horns, screeching sirens, or squealing brakes intruding on nature's sounds to disturb the surfcaster's serenity.

Second, concentrating on a plug soaring through the air and then hitting the water is similar to the archer's following of an arrow as it flies toward its target. While the surfcaster's eyes are riveted on this brightly painted lure, his mind is free to wander.

Third, the motions of casting create a passive attitude considered all-important in meditation. That's true at least 99 percent of the time when no fish is on the other end of the line. Extraneous thoughts and mental images may drift in and out of the surfcaster's awareness without interrupting the physical action. Unless the monofilament line suddenly snarls into a tangled "bird's nest," one cast automatically follows another without interruption.

Fourth, it's a comfortable activity. There's no strain involved in casting out or reeling in a plug. It's an easy, rhythmic action that can be carried on for hours without much physical or mental fatigue. But it's the combination of all four of these elements that produces the transcendental state of mind considered essential for successful meditation.

Performed properly, surfcasting is a kind of ballet. It's similar to tai chi, the traditional Chinese exercise that I tried to emulate—though unsuccessfully—during the ten years I lived in Shanghai and Hong Kong. Both activities combine meditation with a series of not very strenuous movements that flow gently from one into another.

In his illustrated *Tai Chi Made Easy,* Robert Parry claims that these motions can help reduce stress, unleash creative energy, counter depression, and foster self-confidence and optimism. It's hard to make all of those claims for surfcasting, though the hidden benefits are immense.

Eastern mystics and tai chi experts are not the only ones recognizing the detached mental state produced by a repetitious physical activity. Champion athletes speak of the automatic eye-hand coordination required in a sport, and the ensuing moments of higher perception that permit them to perform some seemingly impossible physical feats. They also describe the stopping of time—"an infinite present with everything moving in slow motion"—while performing this feat.

"The experience is one of beautiful isolation," wrote Bill Bradley, the ex–New York Knicks star and former Democratic senator from New Jersey in his pro basketball autobiography, *Life on the Run.* "It's as if a lightning bolt strikes, bringing insight into an uncharted area of human experience."

A dozen years ago I wrote a book about intuition. In it I attributed those sudden illuminating, "I've found it" flashes described by Bill Bradley to the "Eureka factor." The Eureka factor works best for me when I'm surfcasting. The isolation of being the only person on a long strip of sand, or being surrounded by giant boulders, or simply absorbing the sun's reflection on the water is mesmerizing. In this peaceful environment my mind is most fertile, with disparate thoughts and ideas seeming to spring unsolicited out of the sea air.

It's been my experience that ideas for articles and books, including the spark for this one, can hit as hard as a bluefish right in the middle of a cast. That's not surprising. Writing and surfcasting have certain things in common. As one trout-fishing essayist pointed out: "The masochistic urge to wake up in the predawn hours to catch something you ultimately let go is not dissimilar to the quirky yearnings that guide the writing life." Of course, surfcasters are not obliged to release their catch any more than writers are forced to discard their prose.

Most often it is some random thought about nature, or science, or the immensity of the universe that magically surfaces in my mind while I'm surfcasting. Once in July 1997, heaving out my line from atop a massive boulder beneath Block Island's Southeast Light, I felt myself suddenly transported to the boulder-strewn surface of Mars, 120 million miles away. I was actually seeing Sojourner, that little robotic rover, inch its way over the red planet. Of course, just the night before I had been studying those incredibly crisp pictures sent back from Mars by the spaceship *Pathfinder.*

Sounds as well as sights can send my thoughts traveling in unexpected directions—especially when the boredom of repeated and fruitless casts is numbing my mind.

Early one morning an earsplitting clap of thunder sent me scurrying out of the surf. My graphite rod, I feared, could become a lightning rod—which is why surfcasters, like golfers, are scared off by electrical storms. In any case, this loud clap of thunder made me think of an explosion that the old-timers who were on Block during World War II still talk about because it jolted the whole island awake. Walls shook and windowpanes shattered.

Oddly enough, this memorable blast occurred on the morning Germany surrendered. A German U-boat was sneaking past Crescent Beach, when it was apprehended by a navy frigate. The German captain was apparently unaware that the war had just ended and was still trying to pick off American vessels entering Narragansett Bay. Without any warning to the islanders, a geyser filled with black smoke erupted from the sea off the stern of the frigate as a three-hundred-pound dynamite charge blew a hole in the U-boat. The fifty-six Germans aboard were killed instantly. But for years afterward, commercial fishermen were told to give a wide berth to the undetonated explosives sitting on the ocean floor.

Sometimes while swinging my "surfstick" (that awful slang term for a casting rod) in one of my tuned-out states, I'll absentmindedly forget to open the bail, only to have the plug wrap itself around the tip of my pole on the next cast. "Stupid bastard," I say to myself. But then I recall the apocryphal story about philosopher Immanuel Kant holding an egg in his hand while placing his watch in a pot of boiling water to time it.

I can become so oblivious to what's going on around me that I'll wake up to waves slapping precariously against the top of my chest-high waders. That apparently is what happened to Bronx school teacher Ben Lubell, an expert surfcaster who spent his summers on Block Island. Caught in the wildly churning rip on Sandy Point at the northern tip of the island, he apparently wasn't aware that his waders were filling with water. He was last seen waving his rod in the air while being swept away by the surf. A week later his body washed ashore in nearby Cow Cove.

Horrified spectators standing on the sandbar that night of August 23, 1980, thought this skilled surfcaster was merely holding his rod aloft to keep his reel dry. But Lubell had an inordinate fear of drowning and had once told a fishing companion, "If you ever see me out in the boiling surf waving my rod in the air, grab hold of it and haul me back to safety."

Casting for Fresh Ideas

The fifty-three-year-old Lubell was known throughout the island as a fishing fanatic. For twenty-five
summers he went out morning, noon, and night in
pursuit of fluke, flounder, weaks, blacks, blues, bass,
or bonito. "It's not just to catch fish," he insisted. "It's
to watch the sun rise and set and to see the spectacu-
lar clouds." Of course, he loved landing a monster
striper, and frequently caught one of those forty- or
fifty-pound night feeders after everybody else had
given up and gone home. But to give his quarry an
even chance, he filed the barbs off his hooks.

Sandy Point, Lubell's favorite place to fish, can be
scary. The tremendous turbulence caused by the Atlantic Ocean and Block Island Sound pounding in
opposite directions over the two-mile-long sandbar attracts fish, all right. But that wasn't its main attraction
for Lubell. "I like it there," he once told a friend, "because at the northernmost tip of the island I know I'm
breathing the sea air before it has passed through anybody else's lungs." Sadly, Sandy Point proved to be the
place where this venturesome surfcaster drew his last
breath.

Every time I wade into those same swirling waters I
think of Lubell. It keeps me alert. Once, though, those
thoughts were happily broken by a hard jerk on my
line. I was nervously watching the waves break on the
sandbar and not watching my plug, so I missed seeing
the splash. The line went slack. But there was a second, bigger splash, backlit by the low evening sun. This

time the fish was hooked—foul-hooked, I thought, because I could see stripes spiraling crazily in out of the waves.

Hauled slithering onto the beach with my popper snagged in its left gill, the thirty-inch-long striper was barely a keeper. As carefully as possible, I lifted its gill cover to remove the barbs embedded in the feathery red filaments that enable a fish to draw dissolved oxygen from the water.

Once again I was plagued by the same bothersome question: "Should I keep this fish or return it to the ocean?"

There was nothing unique about my ambiguity. Many times it has been noted by sport fishermen that their killer instinct coexists with a catch-and-release softheartedness. The mere act of hauling in this fish had already satisfied any atavistic urge inherited from my hunter-gatherer ancestors.

There was yet another reason for letting it go. Although this four- or five-year-old striper was of legal length, granted four or five more years of freedom it would grow to a size that could give some lucky surfcaster a real tussle. Fish have poor memories, so the fact that it was fooled by my plug wasn't going to keep it from making the same mistake again.

I happily eat fish. So I felt no squeamishness about sacrificing this still very much alive creature for our dinner table. And plucked right out of Block Island's unpolluted waters, it was sure to taste delicious. Nevertheless, I massaged it gently in the shallows while it regained its strength, and then let it swim away, my mouth watering a bit over the missed meal.

Every time a perfectly broiled fillet, garnished with parsley and lemon wedges, is laid out on a plate in front of me, I'm reminded of a letter written by young Ben Franklin after being becalmed off Block Island on a voyage from Boston to New York. A copy of his letter is displayed on the wall of Block Island's Ship-to-Shore bookstore. Wrote Franklin:

> Our people set about catching Cod and hawl'd up a great many. Hitherto I had stuck to my Resolution of not eating animal Food; and on this Occasion, I consider'd the taking of every Fish as a kind of unprovok'd Murder, since none of them had or ever could do us any Injury that might justify the Slaughter. But I had formerly been a great Lover of Fish, and when this came hot out of the frying pan, it smelt admirably well. I balanc'd some time between Principle and Inclination: till I recollected, that when the Fish were opened I saw smaller Fish taken out of their Stomachs: Then thought I, if you eat one another, I don't see why we mayn't eat you. So I din'd upon Cod very heartily and continu'd to eat with other People, returning only now and then occasionally to a vegetable Diet. So convenient a thing it is to be a *reasonable Creature*, since it enables one to find or to make a Reason for every thing one has a mind to do.

Isn't it wonderful how that brilliant, straight-thinking inventor of the lightning rod and signer of the Declaration of Independence could have so easily rationalized away his principles? But when it comes to fish and fishing, we surfcasters are also experts at rationalization. Otherwise, we wouldn't be able to labor so long at the water's edge with so little to show for it.

As we set out at the crack of dawn, or even earlier, in pursuit of our quarry, we "make a reason for it," as did Ben Franklin when he smelled the pan-fried cod placed temptingly before him. We convince ourselves that on this day for sure we'll return home with the prize that will be tastily displayed on the dinner table in the evening. After all, we surfcasters are a dedicated, devout, die-hard breed. More important, we are eternally optimistic.

Camaraderie
Is Catching

*"We catched fish and talked, and we took a swim
now and then to keep off sleepiness."*
Mark Twain (1835–1910),
The Adventures of Huckleberry Finn

S urfcasting isn't only for those seeking serenity.
Seeing the sun's flattened fireball slide silently
into the sea, watching ominous night clouds
scud scarily across the moon's pale face, tasting the
cold salt spray blowing off the wavetops, and all the
rest of those part-physical, part-spiritual sensations
that come while fishing off a beach can also be shared.

True, the camaraderie of having someone else along may interfere with the kind of soul searching I described in the previous chapter. With a friend at hand, it's hard to feel the personal minuteness and powerlessness experienced while wading all alone into a surging sea. And the mere presence of another person to talk to detracts from the oneness felt with nature.

Nevertheless, surfcasting with a friend, spouse, son, or daughter is pleasantly congenial. (I must admit that with four sons and nary a female offspring, the fun of fishing with a daughter is strictly hearsay.) The focus may be on catching fish. But the emphasis is also on companionship, especially if the other person is not seriously infected with the surfcasting bug. The result can be a closer personal relationship, or even being *bonded*, to use that sticky, gluelike word bandied about so freely today. And when the fish aren't hitting, a little light banter with a few tall stories thrown in can fill the void.

My oldest son, Dana, caught the surfcasting bug from me, just as I caught it from my maternal grandfather, though his casting was confined to the shores of a New York State reservoir stocked with perch and smallmouth bass. In addition to his rod, Gramps also carried a heavy silver-headed mountain stick that he used to club to death any sluggish carp that ventured too close to shore.

Dana grew up on Long Island Sound and has been

an ardent saltwater fisherman ever since he was big enough to reel in a flounder. One morning when he and his three younger brothers were still in elementary school they awoke to the thrashing and splashing of an enormous school of blues in the tidal basin directly in front of our house. Thousands of choppers were in the midst of a wild feeding frenzy, chasing bunker and churning the whole cove into a white froth.

Each of my sons, even the youngest (who was only five at the time), had his own casting rod. For an hour they stood side by side in their pajamas on the front lawn hauling in blues. That learning experience, I decided, was a perfectly legitimate excuse for being late to school.

As the boys grew older they accompanied me on trolling excursions around the islands and coves perforating the Connecticut coast. They would rise at dawn—though often reluctantly, still rubbing the sleep out of their eyes. Our refrigerator always contained a few cardboard boxes of lethargic sandworms imported from Maine, which didn't delight my wife, Helen. Moist seaweed was supposed to keep the worms alive (and from smelling) for four or five days. So while I rigged the rods in our Boston Whaler, the boys would pick through the seaweed and toss out any worms that might have expired. Then with the smoky morning mist still clinging to the surface of the sound, we'd troll the sandworms hooked up to Cape Cod spinners.

Some mornings we'd stop to check the half-dozen lobster pots baited with bluefish heads that I had strategically placed around Great Captains Island. On good days we'd return before breakfast with a couple of striped bass fillets to pan-fry with our eggs, and frequently with four or five lobsters to steam for dinner that night.

During the years that followed, the stripers became scarcer and the three younger boys lost interest in fishing, though on periodic trips back home their interest seemed more dormant than dead. Occasionally, I detected a reawakened urge in them to head out early in the morning with me in pursuit of a striper or blue.

Dana, on the other hand, grew into a hard-core surf-caster. Like me, he sensed something almost sacred about angling amid so much natural beauty, though he admitted only to the meat fisherman's desire of catching something edible. But it was obvious that the rough physical contact with an unruly ocean exhilarated him whether we were fishing from the beach or a boat.

Once when we were trolling and I was trying to wax poetic about the mysterious realm of the sea and the strange messages sent from the deep—as might be expected from an Aquarian who is also a writer—Dana shot back disparagingly: "The only message I ever get is from a fish jerking my line, and I haven't heard a word from the deep all day."

These days my surfcasting with him is spent mainly on the boulder-strewn coast and beaches of Block Island. I sold my last boat, a twenty-foot Bertram, several years ago, after deciding it wasn't worth the expense and upkeep. Perhaps an even bigger drawback to the boat was the need to have a second person aboard to help me dock, undock, and especially fish the often rough waters surrounding Block. Helen always assumed I would probably fall overboard if I went out alone. Besides, the throbbing 165-horsepower engine intruded on the peacefulness of the morning or evening, when the fishing was best.

But one morning when we still owned the *Taipan,* as the Bertram was named following our family's five-year sojourn in Hong Kong, Dana and I were drifting and casting plugs lackadaisically a mile off Block Island's Southeast Point. The sea was mirror smooth, so we weren't really expecting a hit. Periodic scans of the horizon with binoculars revealed not a single school to chase.

Those chases, when they occur, can be exciting, even chaotic, especially if two boats are on a collision course, both bearing down on the same school. The idea is to speed full throttle to reach the school first, then cut the engine so the boat coasts silently into the middle of the frenzied fish. It takes split-second timing to get off a couple of casts before the whole school sounds. But if you're quick enough, three or four blues are sure to smash savagely at your plug until one of them is hooked. And with two people casting on opposite sides of the boat, the chances are good for a doubleheader.

Dana and I have had some crazy experiences dancing around the deck trying to keep our lines from crossing as we played a pair of big, wildly leaping blues. *Pandemonium* is the only word to describe what goes on in a boat at such moments. But doubleheaders can be dangerous, especially if two freshly boated blues are flipping around the cockpit with plugs sticking out of their mouths. The sharp barb of a treble hook can end up painfully embedded in your hand or leg. Mark Kauffman, a former *Life* photographer and an old fishing buddy, got hooked in the thumb this way one morning when he was out in the boat with me. An enormous school of blues, something he had never witnessed before, was jumping all around us. He was so determined to keep on casting that he insisted on my cutting his line and taping the loose plug to his hand, but with the barbed hook still buried in his thumb. The tape, he figured, would keep the hook from tearing the flesh. After a few more casts he surrendered to the pain and let me take him to the hospital emergency room to have the hook surgically removed. Of course, by the time we got back in the boat with his thumb neatly bandaged, the fish were gone.

But on this morning with Dana the sea was dead. And the sky was just as empty, with no telltale flocks of terns pointing the way to a school of feeding fish.

Dana was reeling in, and as his plug came wobbling back over the flat sea toward the boat, a stray blue shot up from the deep and grabbed it.

We were using twelve-pound-test line, and the powerful fish took one leap into the air and then started stripping line as it headed for the bottom some forty feet below.

Something strange often happens to a fisherman after a big fish strikes. No matter how seasoned the angler, his two arms miraculously turn into a scale that weighs the wild creature at the other end of the line. "Must be a twenty-pounder," Dana shouted.

Big or small, this baby wasn't going to give up easily. The fish started swimming furiously back and forth under the boat; Dana had to jump around the deck to keep the thin monofilament from chafing against the hull or, worse yet, wrapping around the stern drive.

I finally fired up the engine and tried following the taut line to keep it from snapping. But the fish suddenly reversed course, forcing me to stop the motor and let this lunker swing the boat around with its own power until we were pointing at it again.

The battle continued for thirty minutes before the big blue began to tire. I've read that during a fight, a buildup of lactic acid in the fish's muscles can poison it, and sometimes even kill it. But as this fish began to tire and came closer to the surface, showing us flashes of silver in the translucent turquoise sea, it wasn't about to give up. Dana, too, was beginning to tire. But he desperately wanted to boat this baby, which in his mind had now escalated to twenty-five or thirty pounds.

After another ten minutes the fish was up on top, but still thrashing wildly some twenty feet behind the boat. Every time it jumped, its big head shook, trying to dislodge the treble hooks caught in the corner of its mouth.

Dana continued to gain line until the fish was swimming smoothly alongside and I was able to slip a gaff into its soft belly and yank it into the boat. That blue had fought a gallant fight that neither of us will forget. It weighed seventeen pounds—far from a record but a large blue, indeed. In Dana's recounting of the fight, this blue has been getting heavier and heavier, and may yet set a record before he tires of telling the story.

Recently the two of us spent a less successful summer night together casting from the beach at the Cut leading into Great Salt Pond. Big bass were there, all right. We could hear them splashing, but well out of casting range in the center of the channel. Even more tantalizing were the phosphorescent swirls made by the schoolies feeding close to shore, just a few feet from where we were standing.

It didn't matter what we tempted these fish with—rubber sand eels (Slug-Gos is their trade name), or the old standby blue and white plastic Striper Swipers, or even a shiny metal Hopkins that glinted underwater in the moonlight. Nothing worked. Not even the youngest, unwariest bass among them could be tricked into chasing anything that wasn't made of real flesh and blood.

With stripers all around and nary a strike, it's easy to become a little perturbed, even though this time we knew what the problem was: There were simply too many sand eels in the water for our lures to compete with. In fact, these slender, silvery fish were flipping up onto the beach all around us, trying to flee from the bass. Instinctively, the squirmy little guys preferred dying a slow death on land to being eaten alive in the water.

Flocks of black-crowned night-herons hang around the Cut as soon as it gets dark. They were squawking derisively at our lack of success, or so we thought, all the while strutting up and down the water's edge munching on the beached sand eels.

Why didn't we just pick up a live sand eel, put it on a number two hook, and then toss the still-wriggling baitfish back into the water? That would have meant giving in. And as I kept reminding Dana, whose hunter-gatherer instincts were stronger than mine, the real challenge of surfcasting is to fool a fish into hitting an artificial lure.

Frustrated by our failure to fool even one schoolie, we decided to take a break. We'd brought along an old blanket used for wrapping furniture. Spreading it on the sand, we lay down for a while, watching the moon duck in and out of the clouds, listening to the ruckus raised by the splashing stripers and sqawking night-herons.

The chance to talk to an adult son without the interruptions that crop up at home on an abbreviated weekend visit struck me as almost better than catching fish. We chatted about Dana's job, and the possibility of his belatedly going back to graduate school for an MBA, then making a career switch. We also discussed the not-so-distant day when he and his younger brothers would take over the family property on Block Island. We also carped plenty about those stupid bass that wouldn't bite.

As a parent I always felt lucky that Dana had been a shade too young to get caught in the Vietnam draft. Not long before the fall of Saigon, when I was covering the war there as a correspondent for *Time* magazine, he flew over for a visit. The son of our Vietnamese photographer took him on a tour of the delta. The sight of all the burned-out villages—many of them coastal fishing communities—and long lines of fleeing refugees has never faded from his mind. He also vividly remembers how Vietnamese cooks could make even the lowliest trash fish taste delicious.

Block Island, isolated as it is, had an unlikely, but highly publicized connection with the anti-Vietnam protest movement. Father Daniel Berrigan, the fugitive Catholic priest who became one of the country's most vocal protesters, chose to hide out on Block. When the FBI finally got wind of his whereabouts, it sent over a covey of agents, ludicrously disguised as bird-watchers, to arrest him. All the locals immediately knew that the orange-jacketed, binocular-toting young men were feds. And so did Father Berrigan, who simply came out of hiding to greet them.

The blues and stripers on Block Island, as should now be clear, don't often surrender so willingly. One fall I invited a group of my fishermen friends to come for a three-day assault on the stripers during their annual fall migration. Every October and November the bass from Cape Cod, Nantucket, Martha's Vineyard, and Cuttyhunk pause at Block to fatten up on the island's baitfish before proceeding south to their freshwater spawning grounds in the Hudson River and Chesapeake Bay. A mighty fall migration of surfcasters also descends on the island to intercept them.

I picked the third week of October for what was to be a bachelor party comprised solely of fellow writers and editors, who happened also to be devout surfcasters.

"The time is propitious for fishes," began the invitation letter I mailed to Bob Manning, former editor of the *Atlantic Monthly;* Dick Billings, former editor of the *Congressional Quarterly;* Jeremy Main, then a writer for *Fortune;* Frank White, the retired Paris bureau chief for *Time;* John Williams, a retired reporter for the *Wall Street Journal;* and Don Moser, editor of *Smithsonian* magazine. Moser couldn't make it. My youngest son, Marc, decided to fly up from Dallas and join the group—not because he was crazy about surfcasting, but mainly to hear the wild yarns he knew would be spun by these veteran journalists.

As Nelson Bryant of the *New York Times* once wrote in his "Outdoors" column: "A generous degree of confidence is required to invite friends to angle in your home waters, particularly if you are—rightly or wrongly—regarded as something of an expert." Bryant aptly pointed out, "There's always the possibility during the few days you have decided to play host that the fish you are seeking will not be around or that the weather will be unfavorable."

Both of the aforementioned occurred. When my guests, who had journeyed from Boston, New York City, and Washington, D.C., met at the Block Island ferry terminal in Point Judith, the tail end of a tropical storm was still whipping up the seas. As is usually the case during bad storms, all the ferries had been canceled—partly to spare the passengers a miserable ride, and partly to give the captains and crews a day off.

We then faced the choice of spending a night in the seedy motel across the street from the ferry dock, which featured a flock of noisy parrots jabbering senselessly around an indoor pool, or driving thirty miles south to the Westerly airport, where the commuter planes to Block had already resumed flying. We decided to fly.

Out on the island the weather improved rapidly,

but the storm had apparently sent all the stripers south ahead of schedule. We tried casting from every cove, beach, and rocky promontory on the fifteen miles of fishable shoreline.

At Charleston Beach Bob Manning did catch a puny twelve-inch striper, barely big enough to get its mouth around his plug. At Black Rock I hooked into a huge blue, still hanging around after most of its buddies had headed for warmer waters along the Outer Banks of North Carolina. But after leaping out of a wave, high enough for me estimate its weight at twenty pounds, it wrapped my line around a boulder and broke off. Those were the only two fish we saw during the entire three days. My reputation as a guide was saved only because the hundred or so other visiting surfcasters fared no better.

Our bad luck reminded me of George Bush's well-publicized 1989 fishing vacation in Maine. For seventeen straight days he was skunked, proving that even a president of the United States is not immune to this ignominy. A so-called fish watch was created by the *Portland Press,* which used the picture of a bluefish with a red line drawn through it to chalk up each zero day. Finally, on the eighteenth day Bush reportedly appealed for divine help during Sunday services at Kennebunkport's Episcopal church. Later that morning, to the cheers of the reporters and Secret Service agents, he landed a ten-pound blue.

In our case, the absence of fish neither led to an

appeal for divine intervention nor dampened our party. The hours and hours of futile casting were followed by many more hours of spirited storytelling, fueled by free-flowing martinis, beer, Scotch, and sour mash. Like the fishing itself, the stories dwelled mostly on unlucky encounters experienced at one time or another by these eminently successful journalists.

Frank White regaled the group with his misadventures while escorting Henry Luce, *Time* magazine's founder and editor in chief, around Paris. Much to Frank's chagrin, one of Luce's favorite games was to walk into Cartier's, or some other expensive jewelry boutique, and stir up a buzz of excitement among the clerks by asking to see bigger and bigger diamonds, only to walk out feigning disappointment at the minuteness of the baubles he was being shown.

Frank also described a disastrous meeting he'd arranged for Luce with France's Prime Minister Edgar Faure. *Time*'s editor insisted on using his limited Yale French, while the P.M. stuck to his equally rudimentary Sorbonne English. Their conversing difficulties, according to Frank, were compounded by Faure's cleft palate. Neither man, he recalled, had a clue what the other was saying.

John Williams told how one year when he was Detroit bureau chief for the *Journal,* he had stuck to his guns and refused to adhere to the long-accepted news moratorium on the new car models. But by writing about them in full detail prematurely, he cost his newspaper a bundle in lost ad revenues. Fortunately for John, his bosses in New York refused to cave in to the car companies' cries for his dismissal.

Occasionally the good-natured banter became a little steamy. Dick Billings, a perennial conspiracy buff, had written a book about JFK's assassination titled *The Plot to Kill the President.* He insisted that the sound of several explosions picked up on a tape recorder near the Dallas Book Depository when the presidential motorcade was passing by were not caused by the backfiring of police motorcycles, but came from shots fired by a second gunman.

Bob Manning, who between magazine editing jobs had served as Assistant Secretary of State for Public Affairs under Kennedy, claimed Billings was crazy to have based an entire book on such flimsy evidence.

Determined to get the storytelling back on a lighter track, Manning then acted out an exchange supposedly overheard coming from two senile members of a staid old club he belongs to.

"Good to see you again, old boy," said the first member.

"Ah, wonderful to see you, too," said the second. "But forgive me, I seem to have forgotten your name."

"Quite all right, old boy," said the first. "How soon do you need to know?"

And so it went, late into the night. Our combined frustration at not being able to catch a single striper of keepable size only heightened the camaraderie of the get-together.

This was not the only time I played host and guide when the fish failed to cooperate. During another surfcasting expedition with John Williams and my brother-in-law George Rounds in tow, the weather was about as bad as it gets on Block short of a hurricane. Pelting rain was followed by pea-soup fog. Of course, that didn't keep us housebound.

After a fishless foray to North Point we decided to take a shortcut back over the dunes to the parking area where we'd left my jeep. Trudging blindly through the fog, we blundered into the vast seagull preserve behind the lighthouse established by the United States Wildlife Service. Gulls build their nests on the ground, and suddenly we were being dive-bombed from all directions by furious, shrieking birds afraid that we were going to step on their eggs. It looked like a rerun of the famous scene in Alfred Hitchcock's *The Birds* in which a group of travelers was attacked by thousands of swooping gulls. We had to cover our heads with our yellow slickers to keep the furious birds from pecking our eyes out.

Not all of my guiding experiences ended so disastrously. There were other times with a visitor along when the fish appeared in great numbers. Once while a dedicated trout-fishing friend from Maine and I were taking a quick dip to cool off after an hour of fruitless casting, a few gulls started diving into the ocean around us. Moments later hundreds of blues shattered the water's surface with the violence of an undersea eruption. Swirling and leaping fish were suddenly putting a foamy head on the sea.

We raced back up the beach and grabbed our rods. By the time we returned to the water's edge, baitfish were flying in all directions as if some invisible force were sucking them up from the ocean. The screaming and diving gulls had attracted more seabirds, and they joined in filling the sky with hysterical cries. My friend, who had never tried surfcasting, was immobilized by the carnage going on in the water where we had just been swimming. "Cast!" I yelled. "Don't stand there! Cast!"

He finally let fly with a plug. And by the time the gluttony in the water ended and the birds quieted down, the two of us had half a dozen big blues flip-flopping around in the sand.

I never could convince my friend that surfcasting isn't always so easy.

The Joys
of Fishing Alone

"The nurse of full-grown souls is solitude."
James Russell Lowell (1819–91), *Columbus*

Freshwater fly fishermen accustomed to fighting their way through tangled vines and branches covering a riverbank, or climbing gingerly over slippery boulders to reach a deep pool with the promise of a giant rainbow trout, may consider surfcasting a sedentary sport. And in an odd way it is. With each wave the soles of your waders sink deeper and deeper into the sand until suddenly you are anchored to the bottom and can barely move.

Fishing writer Owen Hatteras (or is that simply a nom de plume suggested by North Carolina's famous surfcasting cape?) once humorously speculated on how if he stood in one spot through an entire tide, he might sink from view. "Maybe someone coming by a day later," he wrote, "would see just a fishing rod sticking up out of the sand."

This fellow Hatteras also offers a whole slew of suggestions for relieving the boredom when the fish aren't biting. "I particularly enjoy disturbing seagulls," he boasts. "The basic beach gull," he adds, "likes to stand up just back of the beach berm. It is facing the wind, relaxed, and watching me, especially to see if I drop my bait. If I turn to look, it shifts its feet and cocks its head. If I walk toward the gull, it waddles away. If I run half-heartedly, it flies a few feet and sets down again. If I run seriously, it takes off and makes a gentle circle downwind before settling onto the beach again."

The best way to launch a large group of beach gulls, he maintains, "is to run at them with arms spread, shouting 'I want to be your friend.' One is treated to a massive display of jump launching, defecating, squawking, flapping, wheeling, and gliding and an eventual landing down the beach."

Of course, engaging in this kind of horseplay to break the monotony of long fishless periods not only disturbs the gulls, but also shatters the solitude that poet James Russell Lowell wrote "is the nurse of full-grown souls."

For me, at least, nothing nurses my soul more effectively than slowly working my way down a deserted beach, casting aimlessly into the surf, all the while drinking in the peace of the morning or evening. My body begins to feel different, as if I'm moving more efficiently and gracefully in unison with the flying plug.

Many of my friends in today's frenetic world confuse being alone with loneliness—a situation they believe should be avoided at all costs. Even in some primitive societies it's virtually impossible to be alone. Natives of Micronesia, I'm told, consider it rude to leave their friends unattended. For this reason, Peace Corps volunteers assigned to Truk and the other sparsely populated islands in that part of the Pacific have complained of never having any privacy.

In our own society we have a similar problem. "Stay in touch," we say, meaning with you and me and everybody else. *Networking* is considered the password to success in business, and for general happiness as well.

What we seem to forget is that solitude provides us all with a rare opportunity to get in touch with ourselves—even, as we surfcasters have discovered, if this involves engaging in a spirited monlogue with the person holding the rod.

Those surfcasting soliloquies may not be as foolish as they sound. The great philosophers—Spinoza, Kant, Schopenhauer, and Nietzsche—all sought inspiration in solitude. So did some of the most renowned composers, poets, sculptors, and painters. But the inspiration that comes from being alone and experiencing the glories of creation—whether you're standing high on a mountaintop or down on a deserted beach—isn't felt only by the geniuses of this world. It hits us all from time to time, including those addicted to surfcasting.

That's not to say that all surfcasters appreciate solitude. It depends on why they're out there alone on the beach. Like every human endeavor, surfcasting involves both internal and external goals. The external goal is to catch fish, to experience the excitement of landing a lunker, and to put food on the dinner table. If you're one of those meat fishermen who go out solely to catch fish, the solitude part may have little appeal.

It does, however, attract the surfcaster whose first priority is the internal goal, which is much more nebulous and harder to define but comes under the general heading of "letting go."

Letting go means calming your mind and wiping away worry. It means allowing joy to enter your being surreptitiously rather than setting out in a determined way to have a good time. But most important of all, it means relaxing and letting the beauty that is happening all around you seep into your being. All of these psychological and physical benefits are part of the surfcaster's quest.

A place of beauty for one fisherman may be a harsh

and hostile environment for another. Consider for a moment the Siberian ice fisherman. He says he's happiest standing alone on a frozen river, swallowed by vistas of white in every direction. It doesn't matter that the temperature is thirty below zero, that he has to warm the worms in his mouth before sliding them on a hook, or that he may die of hypothermia drifting out to sea on a broken ice floe. "The isolation and serenity are worth it," he says. "It's the most peaceful thing a man can do."

For Henry David Thoreau the place for such serenity and reflection was his beloved Walden Pond. As a sometime angler (but not a surfcaster), he described how important it is for all of us to immerse ourselves in nature while the opportunity exists. "Time is but the stream I go a-fishing in," he wrote, choosing the angling metaphor for one of his most penetrating passages about life and eternal matters. "I drink at it; but while I drink I see the sandy bottom and detect how shallow it is. Its thin current slides away, but eternity remains. I would drink deeper; fish in the sky, whose bottom is pebbly with stars."

We surfcasters, like Thoreau, each look for our own Walden, though it be a favorite little piece of a vast coastline. We identify solitude less with our sport than with the place where we are most likely to find peace of mind.

There are ways, I suppose, to seek out such a place systematically. Or you can simply follow a thread that eventually leads you to it. In my case the thread was my twenty-foot Bertram, which on three successive summer vacations took me first to Sandy Hook in New Jersey, then to Montauk Point at the end of Long Island, before it finally led me to Block Island.

It wasn't love at first sight. A dense gray fog practically blotted out the island on my initial visit. But I gradually became smitten with this isolated Atlantic outcropping created by the same glacier that formed Martha's Vineyard and Nantucket some twenty-two thousand years ago. The land is unspoiled and a profusion of wildlife remains. The glacier, in addition to bringing the rocks and soil that created the island, established a bridge from the mainland permitting the animals to cross. Then twelve thousand years ago the ice receded, leaving this speck of land and the creatures inhabiting it surrounded by water. Many of their descendants are still here.

On clear days Block Island looks fractured from afar. There appears to be a missing part between two small humps sticking up from the horizon. Indeed, six thousand years ago it was two islands. On closer inspection the empty space turns out to be Great Salt Pond, a magnificent enclosed harbor with ample anchorages for some three thousand boats, and three well-equipped marinas to accommodate a few hundred more.

This safe harbor for sailors is matched by the island's unsurpassed trolling waters for those fishermen who are not shorebound. The turbulent rip extending for two miles from North Point frequently seethes with surface blues. And at Southeast Point, in the deeper water a few hundred yards beyond the fissured clay cliffs that are being eaten away by wind and surf, lurk larger bass and blues that on occasion will hit an umbrella rig two or three at a time.

But for me the big attraction of Block Island, besides the surfcasting, is its unblemished beauty. The Nature Conservancy feels the same way. It recently designated this tiny teardrop of an island as one of the twelve "Last Great Places" in the Western Hemisphere.

On sparkling summer days an azure sky dappled with cotton-ball clouds is mirrored in the island's 365 ponds—"one for each day of the year" claims a chamber of commerce brochure. Three-hundred-year-old stone walls crisscross gently undulating grasslands and peat bogs, which Irish visitors say remind them of their homeland. Only on Block the fields are fringed with bayberry, beach roses, and white-blossomed shad.

Just by looking at this vegetation, local residents can tell when to expect the stripers' spring run: "They come when the shad trees bloom and the island is covered with a blanket of white blossoms."

So do boatloads of brides and grooms, who—having visited as surfcasters, or just plain tourists—decide to return and take their marriage vows standing before nature's raised altar, high on Mohegan Bluffs overlooking the Atlantic.

Curmudgeon year-round residents claim their island has become too accessible. They still speak with pride about the old *double-enders,* locally built, two-masted, open boats that used to be the island's sole link with the mainland. Skippered by the likes of Solomon Dodge and "Stuttering Bill" Rose, these seaworthy sailing vessels made weekly mail and freight runs to Point Judith. For years double-enders were also used to hunt down swordfish and giant tuna.

Today, ferries carrying one thousand passengers and forty cars shuttle back and forth from the port of Galillee (across the harbor from the town of Jerusalem) over the same twelve-mile stretch of ocean. But this one-hour voyage, according to the chamber of commerce brochure, "transports its passengers back a hundred years in time."

From first appearances that's true. The island's Victorian hotels and inns, with their mansard roofs and wide rocking-chaired verandas, have not yet surrendered to modern moteldom. They have been meticulously preserved, just as has the wildlife inhabiting the open land behind the antique town that is misleadingly named *New* Shoreham. Certain species of plants, like the endangered blazing star, and animals like the American burying beetle still thrive on Block, though they've been extinct for decades on the Rhode Island mainland.

The burying beetle is the rarest and most unusual of all local denizens. It performed a useful service back in the days when the island's farmers fertilized their land with the carcasses of cod, blues, stripers, and mackerel. This two-inch-long insect, nicknamed nature's undertaker, sniffed out the fish carcasses and buried them by digging away the earth underneath. The female then laid her eggs near the remains, which subsequently fed the larvae.

Unlike the turpentine beetles, which periodically ravage the island's Japanese black pines and for which there is no effective pesticide, every effort is being made to encourage the burying beetles to proliferate. A small colony in Oklahoma is the only other known group in existence.

Ornithologist Elizabeth Dickens is credited with launching the island's first conservation movement almost a hundred years ago. Out hunting for her dinner one night, she shot what she thought was a Canada goose only to discover it was a rare black swan. Dickens was so distraught, she dedicated the rest of her life to protecting the island's birds and their natural environment. Today, about one-quarter of the island's sixty-four hundred acres are under conservation, and the percentage is increasing each year.

With so much of this island's natural beauty and wildlife being preserved, and with such clear recognition of the enjoyment they provide, I can't help but dwell on America's ambivalence about using and abusing nature—particularly the oceans. As an ardent surfcaster it distresses me that it took birders like

Elizabeth Dickens, not fishermen, to first recognize our country's need for conservation laws.

Decades ago, ornithologists pointed out the lethal effect of pesticides on bird eggs. Only recently have oceanographers called attention to how offshore dumping is polluting the seas, and how overfishing is endangering numerous species, including the striper. Sensibly, there are now state regulations limiting the size and number of stripers that anglers are allowed to keep during one day's fishing. But the commercial fleets, aided by spotter planes, electronic fish finders, and long-lines of baited hooks that extend for miles, are putting practically every other species in jeopardy.

On Block Island, conservation has taken a couple of recent leaps and bounds for most unusual reasons. As local bonito fishermen know, that lush green twenty-three-acre neck of land forming the northern side of the Cut leading into Great Salt Pond was confiscated by the Drug Enforcement Administration after its owners were caught growing marijuana. Sold to the United States Fish and Wildlife Service in 1994, it's now a bird sanctuary.

The property is not ordinarily open to surfcasters. But it's worth the trouble of obtaining special permission from the Nature Conservancy office to fish there. In late August and early September, eight- to ten-pound bonito can be spotted chasing bait on the surface just a few feet from shore. But they are finicky rascals. The way these speedy fish are able to spurn a

Swedish Pimple or some other shiny silver lure cast temptingly in front of them can drive you crazy. They act as if they know they're swimming in protected waters.

Also in 1994, a locale known to striper fishermen as Lucky Seven Cove because of the ill-fated (and obviously misnamed) powerboat lying wrecked on its shore, was the scene of another unique conservation effort. In this case instead of land or fish being saved, a lighthouse was rescued.

The clay cliff overlooking Lucky Seven Cove was eroding so fast that the powerful Southeast Light perched on its brow since 1875 was about to slide into the sea. But a million-dollar congressional grant, plus matching contributions from conservation-minded islanders, provided the money to put the two-thousand-ton Gothic structure on rails and move it 245 feet back from the cliff. This two-year engineering feat was carried out flawlessly; only a couple of bricks came loose.

Surfcasting at Lucky Seven Cove is exceptional because of all the baitfish hanging around the reef that partially encloses this cove. At half tide a fringe of frothy white foam outlines the reef. The trick is to cast a popper into the foam and then jerk it quickly back toward the beach. Following this procedure will on most days produce a couple of solid hits, and often a sizable blue or striper to lug back up the bluff.

But just getting to Lucky Seven Cove takes considerable agility. First there are 154 steep wooden steps leading down the side of the cliff to descend, which is no mean trick in waders. Then there's about a quarter mile of slippery, seaweed-covered rocks to climb over. Most of my fishing companions refuse to go through this ordeal.

Before the lighthouse was moved, I would occasionally look up between casts and wonder if the red-brick building looming ominously overhead was going to crash down on top of me. At dusk when the foghorn was hooting, its haunting sound seemed to be saying, "Get out of the way."

One evening I took a British friend there to try his hand at surfcasting. His girlfriend came along, and I quickly got the impression that he was keener on her than he was on catching a fish. After listening to the two of them *ooh* and *aah* about the beauty and serenity of Lucky Seven Cove, I decided to take the hint and leave them alone, even though the man had never done any surfcasting before and clearly needed coaching. So I handed him an old casting rod rigged with a rusty Hopkins that I would have been happy for him to lose, and walked around the rocky point to where I was out of sight.

Being of a suspicious mind, I started conjecturing about this cozy couple and what they might be doing. These lascivious thoughts reminded me of a comparison of the compulsive urge to fish and to have sex that I had recently read in a book called *The Habit of Rivers* by Ted Leeson. "At least sex," he wrote, "under ordinary circumstances demands a pause every now and then, and has prudently built in the nuisance of requiring two people. But fishing can go on indefinitely for hours, day after week after month, and you need involve only yourself."

I had often compared the compulsion to fish with gambling. Each cast, it occurred to me, is like another roll of the dice or turn of a card, rife with the expectancy of striking it rich. Or in the case of surfcasting, getting a strike. But I had never considered any similarities between fishing and sex.

I was weighing the validity of these two intriguing comparisons—fishing with sex versus fishing with gambling—when the Englishman came trotting around the point shouting and waving his arms.

Had this neophyte surfcaster managed to hook his girlfriend? I wondered. Or had she gone swimming and been caught in the strong undertow that makes even wading dangerous in Lucky Seven Cove? No, his girlfriend was fine. But when I reached the cove again, flopping around on the sand was a twelve-pound striper.

"What is it?" he asked. Having caught only small brown trout in England, he'd never seen such a large fish, and one with stripes.

I thought he was going to cry when I gently cradled the striper in the surf while it regained its strength, and then let it swim away.

"Why in the world did you do that, old boy?" he

asked incredulously. I explained that stripers were considered an endangered species and the minimum size for keepers in Rhode Island was thirty-six inches. Or so it was at that time. Since then stripers have multiplied so profusely they need be only twenty-eight inches to keep.

L ucky Seven Cove, with its rugged cliffs and protective reefs, is as primitive and wild, and perhaps just as productive for surfcasters, as it was when the Manissean Indians fished this part of the island, which Californians say resembles their breathtaking Big Sur. But for passing ships it has been a magnet for disaster, claiming some fifteen oceangoing vessels.

In 1903 the 137-foot navy tug *Leyden,* propelled by a powerful new sixty-thousand-dollar engine and piloted by a crewman who didn't hear the foghorn, plowed headlong into the reef. The ship's iron hull was sold for scrap.

Three years later the pilot of the navy auxiliary ship *Nero* heard the horn all right, but miscalculated his position and crashed into the same rocks.

Worst of all was the wreck of the steamer *Spartan* in 1905. Her captain's confusion was evident, because he was headed due west under a full head of steam when he plowed into the island. The *Spartan*'s cargo of calico cloth was salvaged and then laid out to dry on the high ground behind the historical society, known ever since as Calico Hill.

Renewed efforts have been made in recent years to warn ships of this particularly treacherous part of Block's coastline. A better lens was installed in the lighthouse, and its bright beam can now be seen by ships some thirty miles away. At the same time a concerted attempt has been made to preserve the wildness of the area and prevent developers from infringing on its natural beauty. As a result Lucky Seven and its adjacent coves have been left untouched. Hard to get to, perhaps, they are nevertheless reachable to those seeking solitude and some of the best surfcasting on the island.

Not every place you pick to surfcast on Block will be this unpopulated or pristine. Even if you come at dawn, the tire tracks of a departed jeep or beach buggy on some of the more accessible beaches may not yet have been washed smooth by the incoming tide. Or the remnants of a late-night picnickers' fire may still be smoldering. There may even be other fishermen already there casting lures from *your* favorite spot. But as Thoreau pointed out in *Walden,* "Solitude is not measured by the miles of space that intervene between a man and his fellows."

7

Beauty and
the Beach

"Come and see my shining palace built upon the sand."
Edna St. Vincent Millay (1892–1950), "A Few Figs from Thistles"

E ven the most successful surfcasters can find an infinite variety of excuses for not catching fish. "Bad tide." "No surf." "Too many weeds." "Sand fleas were eating me alive." "Too windy." "No wind." "No bait in the water." "Too much bait in the water to compete with." "Full moon." "New moon." "No moon." "Shoulda gone earlier." "Quit too soon."

Then there is the excuse that really isn't an excuse at all because it's one of the main reasons for going surfcasting in the first place: "Went for a walk on the beach and took a rod along just in case."

Fair enough. Dawn or dusk, there are few more sensuous outdoor experiences than a beach walk. The squish of wet sand under bare feet. The shifting kaleidescope of scudding clouds. The sight of the low sun setting the surf on fire, or a full moon turning the whitecaps silver, all add to the feeling of being connected to a universe in motion.

So does the abundance of wildlife on even the most pristine beach: an audience of cormorants lined up on a rock; the V-formation of Canada geese honking overhead; the flashing white wings of gulls wheeling and crying, or just hanging motionless in the wind as they watch for some unlucky crab to claw its way out of the water, where it can be plucked from the beach and quickly devoured before a gluttonous rival gull grabs it away.

The beauty of surfcasting is that it leads you to this magnificent, alive place where soul and sea merge.

But the surfcaster's soul requires periodic recharging with bursts of excitement and action, the kind provided when a school of bonito approaches. Bonito are devilishly hard to hook from the beach. The school moves so fast it's usually within range for only three or four quick casts, many times for only one.

On Block Island in late August, the sight of fishermen racing up and down a beach, flinging out small silvery lures while they are still on the run, usually heralds the arrival of these elusive fish, whose Spanish name, given by the conquistadores, means "little beauty." And little beauties they are, with oblique black bands running from the top of their green backs. Because bonito feed voraciously on the surface, and occasionally close to shore, they make themselves subject to this kind of frantic back-and-forth chase.

Block Island's hottest beach for bonito, and for their close cousin the false albacore, is the strip of sand lining the Cut. Surfcasting there is like fishing from the unobstructed bank of a tidal river, except this river was man-made—though only after several aborted attempts to dig a permanent channel leading from the ocean into Great Salt Pond. For two centuries work crews, equipped with just picks and shovels but encouraged with bonus rations of rum, battled the shifting sands trying to keep the channel open. In 1899 they succeeded.

As the tide turns and starts in through the Cut, the bonito may first be glimpsed ripping the surface and rocketing into the air out by the green buoy marking the harbor's entrance. But the green buoy is well beyond casting range.

You wonder, "Will the school move in with the tide that is sweeping baitfish through the narrow entryway to the harbor? Or will the propellers of some power-boat entering or leaving port scatter the fish?" All you can do is watch and wait with rod at the ready.

Best to stand patiently by a shallow pocket in the

beach where the eddying tide will probably bring the most bait. It's not hard to tell if the action is about to begin. First, thousands of tiny silversides dimple the surface, and then with a great hissing sound fly into the air, announcing the bonito's arrival in the water below. This quick shower of bait may not even be noticed by the gulls and terns unless the bonito, like blues and bass, go into a sustained feeding frenzy.

In this case the bonito themselves will burst into view, chewing up the baitfish with their sharp conical teeth. But one thing is certain: These voracious day feeders will vanish as fast as they came, displaying only flashes of silvery acceleration through the sunlit water. Bonito, after all, are members of the tuna family. Streamlined for speed, they have fins that fold back into grooves in their smooth skin, and stiff tails that provide enormous thrust. Suddenly the churning out by the green buoy stops, indicating the school has moved on. Your eyes hopefully scan the wind-rippled surface between the beach and the buoy, looking for telltale swirls or sudden surface eruptions. But a lone grebe swimming and diving for silversides is the only living thing interrupting this monotonously vacant stretch of water. The grebe pops to the surface and stretches its long neck skyward while swallowing a three-inch-long silverside. The stretched neck allows the fish to slide down the bird's elongated throat and into its stomach without getting stuck.

Though surfcasters are eternally optimistic, their

spirits can plummet as fast as a lead sinker if a leaping and splashing school of bonito suddenly disappears from view. Casting continuously into dead water, hoping to intercept a stray fish before the school reappears, isn't worthwhile. Hold your fire. Remember, at any second the school may surface, swirling and jumping just twenty or thirty feet from the tip of your rod.

The bonito's ability to surprise is what makes them so exciting to pursue. You never know when to expect them, or what they'll do after they arrive. I suppose that's why my lawyer and accounting friends—the ones with precise, logical minds—avoid surfcasting for this species, shunning them as if they were fugo, the poisonous Japanese fish that is fatal to eat unless prepared by a specially licensed chef. Trolling for blues with the probability of a fair day's catch is more their speed.

Unpredictability, however, is something dedicated surfcasters are accustomed to. We always arrive at the beach with high expectations even if some old codger greets us with the familiar refrain: "Shoulda been here yesterday. Blues were everywhere." Or still more frustrating to hear: "It was all over an hour ago. The stripers left at sunup." Or in the case of bonito, witnessing with our own eyes an enormous school taking flight just as we arrive, and saying to ourselves, "Too bad we didn't skip the last swig of coffee and get here a minute or two sooner."

As a journalist I'm accustomed to being greeted by variations of this refrain, though in covering tornados, floods, famines, and other natural disasters, it's usually: "You shoulda been here last month or last week," not merely an hour or minute ago.

One morning my son Dana and I arrived at the Cut just in time to see two surfcasters running down the beach trying to intercept a school of bonito before the splashing fish reached the open water of Great Salt Pond. Coming closer we realized both men were hooked up. Their skimpy casting rods were bent into upside-down Us.

Dana and I made cast after cast, trying desperately to catch up with the departing school. Then we stood and watched enviously as these two excited gents attempted to land their leaping and diving fish. The show lasted for fifteen minutes. But in the end the two bonitos won.

We heard the loud *pop* of one line breaking while the fish was still performing acrobatic leaps out in mid-channel. We saw the other bonito wriggle free and swim away just as it was being dragged up onto the beach. Never have I seen two more dejected surfcasters.

Watching their losing duels reminded me of my own first encounter with bonito. It was in Algiers harbor, of all places, during World War II. As a newly commissioned second lieutenant I was assigned to escort five hundred Italian prisoners from North Africa to the United States aboard the liberty ship *John Harvard*. At the end of the voyage the prisoners would be unloaded and deloused at the Hampton Roads army port in Virginia, before being sent to an internment camp in the Midwest.

Allied ships of all shapes and sizes lay at anchor in the pale blue Mediterranean harbor ringed by the gleaming white city. It quickly became apparent that we were engaged in that old army game of "hurry up and wait." For three weeks, while Algiers beckoned temptingly in the distance, we twirled idly on our anchor chain waiting to unload our cargo of Sherman tanks and then take on the POWs, who would be squeezed like sardines into the empty holds.

To break the monotony, a couple of members of the ship's crew rigged crude hand lines to toss into the schools of bonito that we could see chasing herring around the harbor. Once a bonito was hooked, the trick was to hoist the writhing fish up onto the high deck before it shook loose and flopped back into the water, which is what happened every time I tried my hand at it. Only the more experienced crew members succeeded in hauling a few bonito all the way up to the deck, where they were speedily filleted for supper.

But the merchant sailors, I discovered, had an ulterior motive. They didn't care how many bonito got away. Their fishing lines were decoys, used mainly to reel in bottles of "Dago red," as the sailors called the locally produced Italian wine. Bum-boat boys paddled out to our liberty ship each afternoon to swap the wine for cartons of Camels and Chesterfields. Wine, naturally, wasn't allowed on board, so the bottles came camouflaged in souvenir scarves and shirts.

The bonito in Algiers harbor, I discovered later, were members of the blue-backed Mediterranean species, while those showing up at Block Island in late August and early September are of the green-backed Atlantic variety. Both have the same torpedo-shaped heads, wide mouths, and elliptical tails. They also weigh about the same—generally from four to eight pounds.

Pound for pound, bonito are among the fiercest fighters in the sea. That's why it's worth all the watching and waiting on the beach for a school to come into casting range. But then beaches are not boring places to idle away a little time. Not if you stop to consider the myriad living creatures that are there keeping you company, even if you rarely see them.

The fact is, the very survival of most animals dwelling in the sand depends on their being hidden. They must burrow deep enough to be safe from the surf, as well as from the fish that come hunting for food with the incoming tide, and from the birds that forage at the water's edge after the tide has gone out.

Trudging along the beach waiting for a school of bonito to appear, I sometimes play a little game trying to determine how many telltale signs of various hidden creatures I can find. I look for the scribblings in the sand left by a starfish, a hole bored by a fiddler crab, the squirt from a buried clam, or the slightly exposed edge of a sand dollar. And to think that generation after generation of these creatures have been leaving the same marks upon this sand for thousands of years—maybe millions of years if you include their prehistoric ancestors.

Walking along a beach at low tide is about as close as I ever come to feeling my own fleeting existence— sensing the untold minions that came before me, and the minions that will follow, barring some nuclear disaster that destroys the planet. Viewing the seashore's ever-shifting boundary I can also envision the evolutionary process that carved out and continues to reshape this dot of land called Block Island.

Back when the Laurentide ice sheet covered New England, the Atlantic Ocean was some seventy-five miles south of Block and the sea level 350 feet lower than it is today. Then as the glacier melted and receded northward, raising the ocean's level, it left behind the massive deposits of sand and gravel where I go surfcasting. It's an eerie sensation knowing that I am but a temporary trespasser on a strip of shoreline that will keep on changing forever.

In the preface to her book *The Edge of the Sea,* Rachel Carson expressed these same feelings, but much more eloquently. "When we go down to the low tide line," she wrote, "we enter a world that is as old as the world itself—a primeval meeting place of the elements of earth and water, a place of compromise and conflict and eternal change."

Some of Block Island's evolutionary changes are

easy to detect. Sitting unprotected out in the ocean, the shape and constituency of its shores are constantly being altered by wind and tide. A visitor 150 years ago, before the island had harbors, wrote: "The everlasting thunder of the Atlantic shakes the foundation of the land. It rolls on shore from Europe and Africa, till it breaks here."

We surfcasters can see, sometimes even from day to day, how the beaches we fish from are under heavy assault. They lie serenely during calm days then surrender to the sea during storms, as wild winds drive the waves far up on the shore. At the same time, the protective sand dunes are gradually being whisked away by the wind, further exposing the land behind them to the ocean surges. During summer windstorms at Crescent Beach, on the eastern or Atlantic side of the island, I've watched the black iron particles from the dunes being blown together with the silicone grains of sand. Back in colonial days these fine iron particles were separated from the sand with magnets and shipped to foundries on the mainland. The iron particles were also sprinkled on letters to dry the ink before the advent of blotting paper.

In winter, long after the bonito have gone south, so much sand on the island's western beaches (facing Rhode Island Sound) is sucked out to sea that great mounds of smooth rounded rocks are left piled like funeral pyres along that desolate strip of shoreline. These cobblestones were once also exported to the mainland and used for paving the streets of Providence, New London, and New York City.

The most violent seasonal changes wrought by wind and tide occur at Sandy Point, at the island's northernmost tip. Two hundred years ago this vulnerable extremity was connected by a sandbar to a lushly vegetated little outcropping called the Hummock. At low tide during the summer, islanders would walk out to the Hummock to fish, picnic, or pick berries. But the pounding surf not only beat the sandbar into submission and washed away the Hummock, but also demolished three lighthouses before the existing gray granite structure standing guard at the point was erected in 1867.

The surging sea there occasionally attracts vast schools of bonito. Apparently, the baitfish that are tossed helter-skelter by the turbulent water become so disoriented they are easy pickings for the lightning-fast bonito.

According to local legend this place was also easy pickings for a few mean-spirited early settlers who were said to pillage passing ships after deliberately luring them to their doom by giving false signals with their lanterns. It was called wreckin'.

Those stories weren't true, insist the islanders today. On the contrary, the wreck workers were heroic saviors who on one occasion were awarded eight Carnegie Gold Medals for bravery in coming to the aid of a sinking vessel off Sandy Point.

The wreckin' legend nevertheless inspired John Greenleaf Whittier's famous poem "Palatine," about a ghost ship from the Palatinate in Turkey that met its cruel fate off the northern tip of Block Island:

> Into the teeth of death she sped;
> (May God forgive the hands that fed
> The false lights over the Rocky Head!)
>
> Down swooped the wreckers like birds of prey,
> Tearing the heart of the ship away,
> And the dead had never a word to say.

One evening I was wading into this wild patch of water while trying to recall those two climactic stanzas when a tremendous school of bonito appeared right where the *Palatine* was supposed to have sunk. But the fish were tantalizingly just beyond casting range. Unlike the *Palatine,* they wouldn't be lured closer. Not even herculean heaves with my thirteen-foot casting rod, which sent a Swedish Pimple sailing some three hundred feet out to sea, succeeded in catching the attention of these busily feeding fish. That's what makes surfcasting at Sandy Point so frustrating.

The Cut, with its swift-running tide, is about the only sensible place on Block for trying to catch bonito from shore. Sure enough, a few evenings later my beach-walk musings there were interrupted by the sight of several schools of bonito leaping and streaking through the narrow channel. Grabbing my lightest

casting rod, rigged with four-pound-test line and a
tiny silver and blue Kastmaster, I was able to get off
one quick cast before the tumult in the water subsided. This time the school was within easy reach, and
a fish struck so ferociously that the flimsy rod almost
snapped in two.

Line sizzled off my reel so fast, I thought that this
hell-bent bonito was going to empty the whole spool
before I could turn it around. The fish made it to the
middle of the channel just as a lobster boat chugged by.

"Fish on," I yelled. But the boat's throbbing diesel
drowned out my warning shout. Luckily, the boat's
propellers passed harmlessly over my line.

Then another obstacle appeared between the fish
and me. A clump of kelp came floating in toward shore.
Kelp is something surfcasters frequently have to contend with, and I worried that my line would get tangled in its long, streaming fronds. Funny what crosses
your mind in tense moments like this: I was suddenly
reminded that somebody once told me the midrib of
this seaweed is delicious when cut up in salads. It's also
supposed to be rich in vitamin C.

But much closer to my thoughts as the tussle with
the fish continued was the taste of a bonito fillet cooked
over a low charcoal fire—better even than a steak cut
from its giant cousin, the mighty bluefin tuna.

The kelp, too, was swept harmlessly away by the
tide. Now there was nothing but sunset-streaked water
between me and the fish as it surfaced for an instant

and did what appeared to be a taunting little pirou-ette on its tail. A second later it was gone, diving for the bottom. I wondered if this feisty little fellow would ever give up. How long before it was drained of the fury I could feel even through a hundred feet of mono?

The deeper the bonito dove, the more my rod tip vibrated. I started gaining line, an indication that our duel might be coming to an end. But as I'd learned before, overconfidence doesn't pay in a contest with a bonito. A moment later my line went slack, with nothing but the tiny Kastmaster weighing it down. The fish was gone. My first flash of anger gave way to a feeling of defeat for having failed once again to out-wit a bonito.

I reeled in the slack line and walked slowly back down the beach to the Coast Guard station where my jeep was parked. It had been a super evening of surf-casting, even if I had no fish to bring home. My wife, I knew, was hoping to have fish for dinner, cooked over a low charcoal fire on our grill.

Driving back to the house, I saw myself still there on the beach, tussling with that spunky bonito. Only this time it didn't get away. Finally exhausted, it came spiraling up onto the beach, its gills gasping for the oxygen it couldn't extract from the air.

I wondered what excuse I would have given my wife if I had really caught that fish and then let it go. She's heard them all. "Skunked again," I guess is all I would have said.

Thinking Like a Fish

"Nature is full of genius, full of divinity."
Henry David Thoreau (1817–62),
from his journal of January 5, 1856

A few of my surfcasting friends claim you have to think like a fish to catch them. Peering deep into the luminous eye of a just-landed weakfish, I wondered what had been going on inside the head of this speckled beauty that made it go after my bucktail.

Was it simply hunger pangs? Or was there some kind of primitive reasoning process involved in its decision?

Probably hundreds of weaks, as well as bonito, blues, and stripers, have observed this same bucktail and many other artificial lures of mine darting through the water or skimming the waves without even being tempted. Like every surfcaster, I'm sure more fish have spurned my offerings than have been fooled into striking at them. And I'm just as certain that young schoolies are more easily fooled than old lunkers, indicating that fish, like people, become wiser with age.

So it occurred to me that if it really might make my surfcasting more productive to know how fish think, I should bone up on ichthyology, a science that originated with Aristotle three centuries before Christ. My research, it turned out, didn't help much at all.

The fish's brain, I discovered, is similar to the brain of the fisherman trying to outsmart it. Both consist of olfactory and optic lobes, a cerebrum that controls the voluntary muscles and instincts, a cerebellum that coordinates muscular activity, and something called a medulla oblongata that controls the internal organs. The fish's optic lobes are disproportionately large, even though most fish are nearsighted and can't see clearly for more than a foot or two.

But it's the enlarged cerebrum, the so-called seat of intelligence, that presumably gives the fisherman an advantage over the fish. Some people, particularly surfcasting widows who are awakened before dawn by their husbands clomping around the kitchen in their waders, might dispute this claim. You see, the cerebrum supposedly also regulates judgment, willpower, and self-control—the very attributes you'd expect to keep any sensible surfcaster from going back to the same beach day after day without catching a fish.

All that I eventually concluded from my cursory study of ichthyology is that fish have a certain genius that we surfcasters simply don't understand.

Look at their arduous migratory journeys. Vast schools of stripers move up and down the east and west coasts guided by some inexplicable intelligence or internal compass that leads them far away and then back to their birthplace. Those round-trip journeys may exceed two thousand miles. Impelled by a primordial drive to move, stripers are guided and stimulated by celestial signals and by cues still mysterious to man. Some ichthyologists claim the smell of the river they were spawned in is imprinted on their brains, just as the stretch of shoreline that yielded a large fish is imprinted forever on the surfcaster's brain.

Stripers' internal navigation system seems infallible. Nothing stymies them, not the strongest riptide nor the wildest surf crashing against a rocky shore. They venture in and out of bays and estuaries, up and down rivers, transiting even man-made canals partitioned by locks without ever getting lost. They have even been observed swimming up white-water spillways and vaulting flumes as if they were salmon. But unlike salmon, they don't die after getting back to their birthplace and spawning.

The gathering of the stripers at Block Island for the autumnal move south is massive, covering acres of

sea surface. Occasionally, at this time of year I've spotted what I think is the dark silhouette of a big bass
caught in a cresting wave. The fish appears to risk being swept up onto the beach just so it can stoke up
on silversides or sand eels in preparation for the long
swim to the Hudson River or Chesapeake Bay, the two
principal northeastern spawning areas for stripers. I've
been told that even if a four-foot-long striper, weighing some fifty pounds, is caught in a wave and washed
ashore, it will lie calmly on its side waiting for the next
wave, another sign that this fish is no dumb bunny.

Sometimes I'm not sure if it's really a fish I'm seeing in the wave or just a shadow. There's a fine line in
the surfcaster's brain separating imagination from re-
ality. And after hours of fruitless casting, that line can
become even finer with visions of imaginary fish leaping in and out of waves.

It's very possible, I suppose, that similar optical il-
lusions are produced in the brains of fish, which would
explain why sometimes they will strike at an artificial
lure, imagining it to be the real thing, and at other
times they won't touch one. I've seen underwater
videos showing coho salmon following a shiny silver
lure trolled behind a boat. After inspecting the lure
inquisitively, the salmon will either turn away dis-
dainfully or strike hard, indicating that some kind of
decision-making process is at work. Stripers, too, can
sometimes be observed swirling and following a pop-

per, refusing to strike. Other times they will strike the same lure savagely.

My smattering of ichthyology may not have enabled me to think like a striper, but it did reveal some interesting things about these anadromous fish that live comfortably in both salt and fresh water.

Stripers, it is believed, evolved from freshwater perch in the wake of the melting glaciers that gouged out great rivers running into the Atlantic. Because of their landlocked beginnings, these fish still rarely venture more than three or four miles offshore. But being muscular and hardheaded, they are well endowed to cope with the crashing coastal surf. Stripers now cover the entire eastern seaboard from Nova Scotia to northern Florida, though the great horde confine their peregrinations to the seven-hundred-mile stretch of ocean between Maine and the mouth of the Chesapeake Bay.

On their way south the stripers' first stop at Block Island is usually Cow Cove, a rocky indentation at the northern end that got its name from the cows and other livestock that waded ashore there with the first white settlers in 1661. Among the sixteen original families, who incidentally bought the island from the Massachusetts Bay Colony for four hundred dollars, was Trustram Dodge, a professional fisherman from Nova Scotia. He turned striper fishing into the island's first industry.

Over the years generations of Dodges have fared

better there than the bass. Today eight Dodges, including Charlie Dodge, who used to ship his nightly haul of stripers over to mainland fish markets on the eight A.M. ferry, are listed in the local phone book. At the same time, the local striper population, despite recent conservation measures, has shrunk considerably.

Life for many of these fish begins in the headwaters of the twenty-one major rivers that feed the Chesapeake. Thousands of females, each bulging with some half a million eggs, are accompanied there by thousands more mature, milt-laden males. He and she bump heads in their mating dance, while ribbons of her green eggs spew out into the water and mix with his sperm exuded in milky jets of milt.

Within one day following fertilization a tail starts forming inside each egg. And after three days the tail is thrashing hard enough to rupture the egg's outer membrane, permitting the newborn fry to swim free. Few survive. But the quarter-inch infant that succeeds in staying alive is guided by its nascent intelligence to swim openmouthed toward the microscopic plankton close to shore.

Thus commences a voracious hunt for food that will fuel this fledgling striper's growth and may eventually make it—or one of its brothers, sisters, or cousins—mistake my artificial lure for the real thing. But it will be three or four springs before this young fish is big and strong enough to venture forth from the Chesapeake with its schoolmates—a time when I'll most likely will be on the beach at Block, casting expectantly for my first striped bass of the season.

During the spring striper run, I usually head for Black Rock, the boulder-strewn shore at the blunt southern end of the island. My choice of where to start the season is purely psychological. It's just that from this particular casting area I can make out the dim outline of Montauk on the horizon, and seeing this distant point of land, as I'll explain, raises my hopes of a strike.

You see, even if I can't think like a fish, I keep trying to put myself in the fish's position. Since Shagwon Reef off Montauk is the last feeding ground for a striper traveling north to Block Island, I figure the poor fish will be famished after crossing twelve miles of open ocean to where I'm casting. And if it's really hungry, it's all the more likely to lunge at my plug.

Of course, in early spring it's hard to know just where the stripers are in their northern migration. It depends partly on their size and age. First will come the small schoolies, then the middleweights, and finally in late May the ponderous patriarchs and matriarchs of forty, fifty, and even sixty pounds. But where they all are during any given week, I'm not sure.

It often occurs to me at the start of a new season that I might be overeager, jumping the gun (or rod) before the first bass have arrived. They could still be moving en masse, I think, up the Jersey shore, past the gambling casinos at Atlantic City. Or perhaps they've paused for a nap at Sandy Hook. Stripers do indeed slip away from the school they are traveling with to rest. But not as soundly as blackfish, which conk out on the bottom practically snoring. Stripers are less vulnerable to attack in their somnolent state because they can't close their eyes—another bit of information gained from my cursory study of ichthyology.

The bass, of course, could be closer to Block, but not yet finished dodging tugs and barges passing through the polluted waters of New York Harbor on their way into Long Island Sound. Or they might be taking the ocean route and swimming past Fire Island. Wherever they are, I'm feeling confident. And why not? It's the beginning of a new season.

This wasn't always so. For a while overfishing had driven Atlantic stripers to the brink of extinction. Not too many years ago I had little hope of catching one all year. We surfcasters blamed the commercial fishermen, who in turn cursed the government, which blamed the foreign fishing fleets for invading our waters with sophisticated equipment and canning ships. But passage of the Striped Bass Conservation Act by Congress in 1984, followed by a series of state moratoriums plus more stringent size and catch limitations, produced a remarkable resurgence of the species—proving that we humans, even after messing with Mother Nature, are sometimes smart enough to patch things up.

Knowing of the striper's recent resurgence doesn't keep my confidence from ebbing after countless casts. I'm finally convinced that the stories of the striper's comeback are pure hype. "One more cast," I say to myself, when out of nowhere a schoolie grabs my plug.

I can tell it's no keeper, so I loosen the drag and let it run. Big or small, the first striper of the year is always exciting and I play with this little guy until it's lying exhausted on the beach with the treble hooks of my blue and white popper snagged in both its mouth and left gill.

It's only eighteen inches long, which makes it approximately four years old, perhaps on its first northern junket. As gently as possible I remove the hooks and place the lucky fellow, dorsal-fin up, back in the water. It makes a few unsteady attempts to swim, and then darts away.

Very possibly it will make the same mistake and get caught again during the next dozen or so years before reaching full maturity and a lunker weight of fifty pounds or more. Judging from statistics provided by the American Littoral Society, stripers don't have very good memories. Otherwise, why would the thousands that have been caught and tagged by members of this coastal conservation organization get hooked again? But many do. A few of the two-time losers have even been hauled in by the same person, and in precisely the same place, indicating that striper and surfcaster alike are creatures of habit.

The memory mechanism is obviously one part of the brain where we surfcasters outshine our quarry. We can recall just about every detail of every catch.

The fight a fish put up, the exact spot where it was caught, the time of day, tide, and weather conditions. Only the fish's length and weight tend to become a little fuzzy in our minds, growing bigger as the years pass. And, I might add, that's especially true of the ones that got away.

Of course, mounting a fish is one way to keep it from growing posthumously, though a talented taxidermist can add to the illusion of size by prying open the mouth and curling the tail so the fish looks like it's about to leap off the wall. There was one striper caught on Block—a 70.5-pound monster that set a Rhode Island record and needed no helping hand from a taxidermist. This beauty was caught by Joe Szabo at Southwest Point on a windy November night in 1984. "The seas were horrendous," recalls Szabo, who used to supplement his income by selling his surfcasting catches, before buying a boat and becoming a full-time tuna and swordfisherman. "That bass hardly fought at all. Picked up my eel and ran right up on the beach with it"—an unusually docile striper, and a disappointing tale for a record fish.

The big bass now hangs on the wall at Rebecca's Take Out for all to admire. Of course, stories of the desperate fight it supposedly waged have grown into a marathon battle with Joe almost being dragged out to sea.

Rebecca, it should be explained, is not the owner of this popular fast-food restaurant, but the name of the temperance statue standing outside in the middle of the town's main intersection. The statue's full name is *Rebecca at the Well,* and she was placed in this strategic spot in 1896 by members of the Women's Christian Temperance Union. Their thought was that everyone passing this gleaming white statue, a figure of obvious purity, would be inspired to drink more water and less whiskey.

By the same token, I suppose the monster striper on the wall at Rebecca's Take Out was put there to provide a little inspiration for those surfcasters stopping by to fortify themselves with a cup or two of hot coffee in preparation for a cold night on the beach. However, neither the stuffed fish nor the statue proved to be of sufficient inspiration for some of the more senior surfcasters, who keep a flask in their tackle box just in case the cold seeps into their old bones.

But then Block, like so many other islands, has never been an oasis of sobriety. Its insularity may even encourage tipsiness, especially on stormy days when both ferry and plane service to the mainland are severed. And as so often happens during foul weather, the stripers and blues are driven offshore, forcing the visiting surfcasters to take refuge in the Yellow Kittens or Captain Nick's. At these two bars, the frustrated "bassaholics," as the islanders call them, have been observed engaging in such nuttiness as arm-wrestling contests with steins of beer balanced on their heads.

It doesn't take a storm to loosen up the local gentry.

At lunchtime each day, many of the island's masons, carpenters, and plumbers can be found bellied up to the bar at the Beachhead, which may explain such local home-building oddities as the number of hot-water faucets connected to cold-water pipes. So if you're taking a hot shower on Block Island after a strenuous night of surfcasting, remember to turn on the faucet marked C.

Many of the local lobstermen, swordfishermen, and other seafaring folk also frequent the Beachhead, and occasionally with more serious consequences. After a liquid lunch there one of the ferry captains ran his vessel aground coming into Old Harbor. That would have been forgivable in high seas, because the opening between the two breakwaters is treacherously narrow. But on this calm afternoon, while the passengers and crew watched in disbelief, the captain jumped overboard and waded ashore, leaving everybody stranded.

On a still more serious note, the mayor—or first warden, as the island's top governing official is called—was indicted for rape in 1996 after a drunken night at the Yellow Kittens, which he owns. To make matters worse, he stubbornly refused to withdraw from the election, which he figured he couldn't lose because it was imminent and he was running unopposed. The island's reputation was saved when the jolly young woman who drives the school bus ran as a last-minute write-in candidate and won.

Election day, incidentally, coincides with the height

of Block Island's fall striper run. And as might be expected, with the arrival of the big schools of bass come swarms of surfcasters. The ferries, which ordinarily arrive with some forty cars and trucks, instead disgorge a parade of vans, jeeps, beach buggies, RVs, and other four-wheel-drive recreation vehicles, most of them with rod holders welded to their front bumpers and Styrofoam coolers filled with frozen mackerel and menhaden strapped to their roofs.

If past experience is any indication, there's no telling who'll outsmart whom, the wily fish or the well-outfitted fishermen. Some seasons the stripers skunk the surfcasters, showing complete disinterest in every plug, piece of shiny metal, or—would you believe?—chunk of mackerel, menhaden, or live eel tossed in their direction. Other years, walk along the beach at dawn and you'll see the silver and black corpses of forty- and fifty-pound bass littering the sand.

Southwest Point, favored by the summer influx of surfboarders because of its long rollers, is also the beach of choice for the fall invasion of surfcasters. Local inhabitants, however, refer to Southwest Point as the Lumber Yard. In bygone days so much dunnage was dumped overboard by passing freighters that plenty of sturdy planks for building homes could be picked up on this beach. Today it is more often uprooted telephone poles and dock pilings that wash ashore there.

No doubt about it, in the fall the biggest, strongest stripers also seem to congregate at Southwest Point, their last stop on Block Island before continuing southward. By sunset a veritable village of vans is parked up on the bluff overlooking the ocean. Then as darkness descends, campfires flicker on the beach, while crowds of fishermen can be dimly discerned wading almost hip to hip out in the crashing waves.

When surfcasters converge in vast numbers like this, not only is the serenity of the place shattered, but the night degenerates into a gang-casting contest with snarled lines and snagged plugs. And if by chance you hook up with one of the lunkers that is cadging a last meal in these waters before moving south, you'll have to duel with it in a crowd of agitated fishermen. All of them will fiendishly start flinging plugs over and around you, assuming that the fish you're hooked up with is not a solitary striper, but part of a big school.

A school of hungry bass doesn't have much chance against an army of surfcasters lined up on the beach in almost military formation. A shower of wood, metal, and plastic lures will greet the feeding fish. Ten, twenty, or thirty rods will suddenly bend in unison, marking the start of a slaughter. A few fortunate bass may break off, eliciting some fancy cussing on the beach. A few more may wriggle free while being pulled up onto the sand, unleashing even angrier outbursts. But the end result is the mass murder of a migrating school of stripers, one of the ugliest sights in surfcasting.

Adventures in the Dark

"When it came night, the white waves paced to and fro in the moonlight, and the wind brought the sound of the great sea's voice to the men on the shore."

Stephen Crane (1871–1900), "The Open Boat"

Casting blind into the inky blackness of night adds challenges hard to imagine. There's no watching the plug sail out over the surf, to see if it went where it was aimed or died in flight, just as there's no following its return path as it pops and wobbles back though the waves to where it can be lifted out of the water. And if the lure succeeds in doing what it's supposed to do, there's no seeing the quick splash of a blue or striper making its lunge. Wrapped in darkness, the surfcaster depends on a sensitive touch and sharp ears to tell him these things.

The whole ritual is different for the night fisherman. He starts by jiggling the rod gently before uncorking a cast. A little slack in the line assures him that the plug isn't caught on the tip. Then, swinging the rod forward, he hears the monofilament peeling smoothly off the spool as the plug flies away into the night.

Knowing precisely when to close the bail takes practice and an innate sense of timing. Crank too soon and the plug will stop in midflight, snapping even twenty-pound-test line if the lure is big and clunky enough. Wait too long and ringlets of snarled line will pile up around the reel, or worse yet, wrap themselves around the open bail, making retrieval impossible.

If this happens there's no alternative but to back up onto the beach and pull in the line hand over hand to rescue the plug, before snipping off the resulting bird's nest of tangled monofilament. While performing this delicate operation at night, it's best to use a sand spike to hold the rod upright and keep grains of sand from getting into the reel's gears.

Of course, doing all of the above in the dark is a lot easier said than done. As a diurnal creature, your eyes are accustomed to color and depth, causing you to grope around in the dim monochrome of night.

Besides, the hip-deep water sloshing around your waders is making you tired and cold. The once-lilting sound of the sea singing in your ears has turned into a tiresome refrain. So has the sound of the retreating surf sucking hard at the rubber feet of your waders planted in the sand, making it difficult to stay upright. But this spot is *your* safe little universe and you'd better stand fast.

On moonless nights the emptiness out beyond is a black hole full of mystery and danger—but barren of fish, you're sure, after numerous casts. I've often thought how helpful it would be if stripers and blues had light-generating capabilities like the bioluminescent deep-sea fish discovered by scientists in the sunless waters thirteen thousand feet below the surface in Bermuda. One of these fish was observed shining a two-foot beam of light at the prey it was about to devour. If bass and blues could do this, at least we surfcasters would know where our targets of opportunity are at night.

After an hour or so of casting blindly into this black hole, you're sure it's a dead sea. Then suddenly from deep in that cosmos comes an unmistakable yank. There is indeed life out there.

Just as the dark exaggerates distance, so does it magnify the strength of the fish you are connected to. At night a twenty-pound striper pulls like a forty-pound striper, and the fight it wages feels far more furious than ever in daytime. And if you win this fight, the elation of landing what you assumed is a lunker won't be diminished one bit when you see a less-than-lunker-sized fish flopping on the beach. It's still a victory. The night has yielded up a prize.

On Block Island there is a cult of night surfcasters who relish the peacefulness of their dark world, lit only by the stars and moon. They enjoy hearing the unseen *plop* of the plug, the pounding of the surf; they love feeling the strike of a powerful bass. And when they go home and happily crawl back into bed, they don't seem to mind the wet sand still clinging to their legs.

These night owls know that the big stripers are among the ocean's most voracious nocturnal feeders, and it's these big ones they're after—not the fifteen or twenty-pounders. Especially in the spring, when the moon beams down on the slapping tails of thousands of menhaden, the forty- and fifty-pound bass will go into a frenzy. So will these super-serious surfcasters, who use live menhaden as bait to hook one of the lunkers. The foot-long mossbunker, as they're also called, are too oily and bony to be eaten by humans. But for bass, and for blues, too, they're sirloin steaks.

To be truthful, the surefire baits at night are live eels. Only in a moment of desperation did I stoop to use one of those slimy, wriggly sea snakes, and that was a secret I kept for years. Frozen mackerel chunks or squid are also highly effective in the dark. But I deplore them, too.

One night while idly shining a flashlight into the shallows under the ferry dock, I spotted a school of stripers gorging themselves on a hapless school of ink-squirting squid. But an artificial lure tossed into the midst of this mayhem failed to attract any attention at all. And why would it? Those bass were enjoying a calamari banquet.

Lights, however, tend to scare stripers away. That's why I rarely bring one along, having already scouted out the beach I'm going to cast from at night. It's worth remembering that the reconnaissance for night fishing should be done by day, and preferably at low tide. Under the ocean's surface are shifting hills, ridges, and gullies formed by repetitive wave action; they often attract fish. If, for instance, you find a break in a sandbar paralleling the shore, you've hit upon a likely place to return to that night.

Casting in the dark from a previously unexplored beach is foolhardy, if not downright dangerous. Too many underwater holes to fall into, or rocks sticking up out of the water to stumble over. Besides, darkness will dramatically alter the appearance of even the most familiar stretch of shoreline. It may be difficult to find the spot you're looking for if you haven't scouted it out in advance.

My favorite night-casting area on Block Island is West Beach, the mile or so of gravelly coastline running from the dump—or transfer station, as it's been more tastefully renamed—to the lighthouse at North

Point. In a few places this beach drops off steeply, but the footing is secure and there aren't many seaweed-covered boulders to snag a plug on. On crystal-clear nights the lights of Watch Hill, a Rhode Island summer resort, twinkle reassuringly on the horizon, vying with the sprinkling of bright stars shining overhead.

Astronomers may insist that these glowing pinpoints in the night sky are globes of burning gas millions of light-years away. But when I'm surfcasting and stop to look up, I see within those constellations the same configurations of birds, beasts, and fish identified in Manissean folklore centuries ago. The Block Island Indians believed that these mythical animals populating the great black dome that encapsulates the earth between sunset and sunrise were guardians of the night. And they considered them friends.

At times when I'm tired of casting and lie down on the beach to rest my back and arms, I study the stars and, like a child connecting the dots in a drawing, see how many of the animals described by the Manisseans I can create with my mind's eye.

But the mind's eye can also play weird tricks on a surfcaster at night. The darkness has a texture that gives things more heft. An ordinary wave may appear as a towering wall of water, threatening to knock down whatever's in its way. A boulder breaking the surface at low tide may assume the shape of a beached whale. And when the wind is strong and the billows break and foam, the phosphorescent water swirling around your legs looks like liquid fire.

Even under a full moon, the surf and the flotsam it carries up onto the beach can appear ominous, conjuring frightening thoughts and images that are hard to dispel. You can tell yourself that the night is beguiling, full of mystery, and perhaps a little adventure. And that there is really nothing to fear. Yet a moment later some eerie, unidentifiable object catches your eye.

One night while casting on West Beach, I spotted bobbing up and down near shore what appeared to be the murky outline of a waterlogged corpse. All I saw at first were two large eyes protruding from a half-submerged head. But that was enough to ignite my wildest imagination. And not without reason.

Throughout Block Island's long history of sea disasters, it was on this particular beach near the North Light where the bodies most frequently washed ashore. The local newspaper, in fact, keeps harking back to the 1907 sinking of the paddle wheeler *Larchmont,* and always with the same set of ghoulish photographs showing some forty or fifty frozen corpses—"resembling ice sculptures in various postures," according to the captions—being hauled from away from here in a cart. Additional corpses kept fouling the beach for days. But for forty-three years the death toll remained unknown, because the passenger list had gone down with the ship. Finally, in 1950 the surviving quartermaster revealed that 332 people had died on the *Larchmont*, establishing it as the worst sea tragedy on this side of the Atlantic prior to the sinking of the *Titanic.*

I tried to resume casting. But the sight of that head bobbing in the surf triggered another, even more gruesome memory, because it involved the missing body of a friend. The woman was flying on a commuter plane along with six other passengers, the pilot, and two dogs when it vanished without a trace in the fall of 1989. The weather was clear. No "mayday" message was heard. Had the sea just swallowed them all up?

A few days later the corpses of the two dogs floated ashore right where I was casting. However, a sonar search of the ocean floor failed to detect any signs of the plane or its occupants. Several weeks went by before a fishing vessel, dragging for flounder off West Beach, snagged a few pieces of the plane in its net. But the fuselage containing the bodies of the passengers and pilot wasn't recovered until spring.

Had there been another shipwreck or plane crash? I wondered as my eyes probed the murky outline of this corpse floating in the water. Still, my curiosity was overcome by the repelling sight of the two eyes peering out at me. I had no desire to wade back into the water for a closer look.

Instead, I packed up and called it quits for the night. Then as I was leaving a wave carried the whole hulking corpse clear up onto the beach. To my relief it wasn't a human body, but the bloated carcass of a drowned deer. "One less deer," I decided on the way home, "is hardly a tragedy on an island plagued by Lyme disease."

Even on calm, uneventful nights, it takes an insomniac surfcaster to keep wading through the shadows on a quest for stripers that often turns into what I've heard called "a pilgrimage of solitude." Naturally, night-fishing forays are not sacred journeys, as the word *pilgrimage* implies, but they do produce revelations and insights that don't readily come to mind in daylight—thoughts about infinity, eternity, and your own minuscule place in God's grand scheme of things.

But there is a physical price to pay for casting far into the night. For one thing, you are upsetting your biological clock—the tiny cluster of nerve cells in your brain regulated by light and dark. Everything in your body, scientists warn, can be adversely affected, from your heartbeat to a normally upbeat outlook about catching a fish. In any case, darkness can be depressing, especially when the stripers act as if they're on strike instead of striking.

The ancient Greeks, who knew a lot about angling (*ankos* means "barbed hook" in Greek), had a mythological explanation for the depressing aspects of night. They believed that the goddess Nyx, who swept across the sky at the close of each day trailing a black star-studded veil, was an accomplice of evil. This wasn't surprising, since she was the daughter of Chaos, and among her children were Doom, Pain, Strife, and Sorrow—some of the many afflictions it's possible to suffer surfcasting at night.

An hour before daybreak, I've found, is the most beautiful as well as the most productive time to fish for stripers. The moon, which was brushing by the stars overhead a little earlier, is now a deep orange and ready to set. Best of all, you know that the blackness leaking out of the sky will soon be replaced by a deep shade of purple. And if it's cold, you can now look forward to the sun's first warming rays.

This change from dark to light also affects the biological clock of the fish. As noted by the ichthyologists, there is a sudden upsurge in the speed of their swimming at sunrise. But this is hardly news to surfcasters, who are used to seeing blues and bass sending up showers of spray as they streak back and forth on the surface gobbling up their breakfast. Plopping a plug just ahead of one of these fast-moving fish will, if you're lucky, produce a silvery explosion followed by a wrenching yank on the rod.

From my experience, the most likely place on Block for a dawn encounter with a striper is Mansion Beach. Heading north from town, it's the last smooth sand on the Atlantic side of the island before you reach the cliffs and boulders of the cove called Pots and Kettles.

Later in the day Mansion Beach becomes a playground for swimmers, surfers, and toddlers building sand castles with toy pails and shovels. And I feel compelled to add, for a scattering of spear fishermen, whom I deeply resent when they emerge from the surf in their skintight wet suits, lugging a fifty-pound striper impaled on a steel shaft. That's one less lunker left for us surfcasters to catch. As the late Dr. Henry Bigelow, the father of modern oceanography, once sagely remarked: "If you take something away, it isn't there anymore."

But at dawn this beach is the private domain of the surfcasters. Almost every summer morning they can be seen sending their plugs flying toward the deep holes in close to shore, where stripers often congregate on an incoming tide. Blues, blacks, and an occasional triggerfish will also show up, making this stretch of shoreline even more popular for casting.

Another attraction, at least for me, is Mansion's storied past. Some of the old-timers, who find wading on the smooth, gently sloping sand bottom easy on their aging legs, have regaled me with tales of the white wedding-cake-shaped mansion that gave the beach its name.

It was built in 1889 by Mrs. Edward Searles, the widow of railroad tycoon Mark Hopkins. Reputed to be the wealthiest woman in America, she hired Harry Vaughan, already famous for having designed the National Cathedral in Washington, D.C., to be her architect. The result was a magnificent beachfront castle made of wooden blocks hand-painted to look like marble. A recent architecture book described it as "the most academic re-creation of Palladianism in America since days of Thomas Jefferson."

Mrs. Searles selected this spot, expecting the clear salt air would be good for her health. But she died shortly after the mansion was completed. Successive owners let the imposing structure fall into disrepair—until Prohibition, when it returned briefly to its former glory as a nightclub and speakeasy. A fire in 1963 left only the stone foundation. Surfcasters walking down to the beach in the dark must now be careful not to stumble over it.

At dawn the horizon at Mansion Beach reaches all the way to Portugal, or so (I was told) Mrs. Searles used to say. The rising sun turns the glowing sea as red as molten iron, making the sudden strike of a blue or striper all the more unexpected. Yet that's when it often happens.

Out of the fiery surf comes a spark of silver. But beware. One quick swipe and the fish may be gone. "Reel fast," you remind yourself. "Keep plenty of tension on the line." That's not easy. Mansion's heavy surge will send a hooked fish tumbling toward shore with enough speed to produce a lot of unwanted slack. And in that churning water you won't know until you finally bring the fish in whether it's still hooked.

Early one morning at Mansion I found myself

fighting what felt like a record blue. It apparently missed my plug with its mouth and, swirling for a second strike, caught its tail in one of the treble hooks. I've never had a fish fight with more fury. Without a hook in its mouth to help me turn it around, the blue headed straight out to sea, almost emptying my reel. With only ten-pound-test line, it took twenty minutes before I was able to tire that fish and drag all eighteen pounds of it up onto the sand.

Some surfcasters claim that landing a foul-hooked fish brings luck, while others believe it's a bad omen. Either way, that plump blue became the pièce de résistance at a dinner that night for us and ten of our friends.

One of the old-timers who used to surfcast on that beach and remembered the mansion before it burned was Fred Benson. Known as the New Shoreham Striper Connoisseur, Fred was for years recognized as the island's best bass fisherman. That was after he and State Senator William Lewis set a record one night, hauling in eleven lunkers, ranging from twenty to fifty pounds, in one hour.

Benson became Block Island's biggest celebrity, always riding in the grand marshal's car in the annual Fourth of July parade and becoming the subject of one of those "My Most Unforgettable Character" articles in *Reader's Digest.* But his fame didn't stem from his surfcasting skill, nor from the fact that for many years he was Block's only black resident. He was known for his extraordinary kindness to children, and for his many years of unstinting public service.

Arriving as an eight-year-old orphan in 1903, he labored from dawn to dusk, helping his adopted parents farm. Later he taught school, served as police commissioner, led the rescue party that salvaged the cargo from the sunken freighter *Essex* when it ran onto the rocks off Southeast Point in 1941, was five-time president of the chamber of commerce and vice president of the blood bank, and at ninety-five was still the island's registrar of motor vehicles. Following his death at the age of 101, the public pavilion at the main bathing beach, where Fred liked to fish at night after all the swimmers had gone home, was named in his honor.

Unlike most surfcasters, who keep their favorite spots secret, Fred was a fount of fishing information. He would tell anybody who asked where the stripers were feeding and what they were hitting. If any of these questioners wanted, he'd take them along on one of his nightly forays. "Fred Benson of Block Island knows as much about taking bass from the surf as any man on the Atlantic Coast," reported the *Providence Journal*.

Fred, of course, was just one of many islanders who during spring and fall bass runs worked by day and fished at night. Many of the local tradesmen, store clerks, and town officials still do. While their wives and children snuggle comfortably in bed, these hardy souls stand for hours in the numbing cold ocean with cracked, bleeding fingers, broken lines, and salt-seized reels, trying to tempt a striper into striking.

Sometimes they keep right on casting until the first rays of sun and the wafer-thin outline of the dissolving moon collaborate to cast a little light on the raven-black sky. They fight off fatigue because nobody wants to quit without a fish to bring home, and thus prove that enduring their ordeal was worthwhile. But they find it hard to keep from dozing, even with the hoarse squawk of the night-herons and the wailing horn of the "hooter," marking the Middle Ground between Block and Montauk, sounding in their ears.

Then a burst of salt spray will slap them in the face, jolting them awake with fresh resolve to catch a fish. Often they don't, which further mystifies all those who fail to see how seeking a fish in a surging sea under the moon and stars can offer more nourishment for the soul than the stomach.

The Last Bass

"It's always the biggest fish I caught that got away."
Eugene Field (1850–95), "Our Biggest Fish"

Ever since colonial days when the first surfcasters stood on the beach hurling heavily weighted hand lines out into the waves, followers in their sandy footsteps have returned home with sad tales of the big one that got away.

This is not to say that fly casters pursuing finicky trout with featherlight flies don't have heart rending stories to recite about the fish they almost caught. But their fishing is as different from surfcasting as badminton is from boxing. And so are their stories.

Maybe it's the bigger quarry we surfcasters pursue,

or the heavier tackle we use (which requires more muscle than finesse), or the turbulent seas we must often battle against that explain the higher drama of our postmortems. For sure, everything involved in the kind of fishing we do is on a bigger scale, including the whoppers we tell. Some may even be true. Well, almost true, like the tale I'm about to tell.

It was late November, with the holidays looming, when I thought how wonderfully different it would be to set down on our Thanksgiving table a plump baked striper instead of a turkey.

Despite a few early cold blasts blowing down from Canada, I decided there must be at least one lunker bass left. One that hadn't yet gone south for the winter. Stripers, I knew, are very tolerant of temperature changes. So while the sea had already dropped below fifty degrees, I figured some hardy old cow or bull bass was possibly still foraging for food in the surf at Block Island.

The "Go Fish" columns in the *Block Island Times* had already stopped appearing, an indication that my chances of success were slim. This column usually errs on the side of overabundance. It describes so many fantastic catches that unsuspecting readers might think they had better hide in the beach plum bushes to keep the blues and bass from jumping out of the surf to attack them. But then the "Go Fish" column is written by a New York lawyer whose hobby is fishing, and everybody knows how good lawyers are at making claims that can't be challenged in a court of law, much less in a weekly newspaper.

There was another discouraging sign. The week-end invasion of blue-collar surfcasters from the factories of Providence, Pawtucket, and New London had slowed to a trickle. Ordinarily, the fishing fever brought on by the great southward-bound schools of stripers is so contagious that these workers would show up en masse on Friday evening, fish until dawn, sleep sporadically on the beach on Saturday, then surfcast again from dusk right through Sunday dawn before heading back to the mainland. Only a few diehards were still coming, an indication that the fever had subsided and that they, too, felt the striper season was finished.

Before finally deciding to defy the odds and seek my Thanksgiving striper, I dropped by the Twin Maples tackle shop to consult with its proprieter, Mac Swienton. He had already begun his winter ritual of repairing rods and reels for the next season. But Mac wasn't entirely bleak about my chances. Yes, a few big bass had been spotted off the breakwater at Old Harbor. And a fifty-pounder had been caught just a couple of nights ago at Southwest Point.

Only a smattering of the less popular lures remained on his wall display. Summer's tempting array had been almost picked clean. I bought a big green bottle-nosed plug that nobody else wanted, evidently because it looked at least ten or eleven inches long and pretty clunky to cast. But a humongous plug might just attract a humongous fish—a hearty meal for a hungry striper setting off on an arduous journey.

I also purchased a bottle of Uncle Josh pork rinds. If only a few bass were still chasing baitfish around the island, it occurred to me that dressing up this ungainly wooden plug with a strip of real animal skin fluttering off the back hook might make it more seductive.

Before I left Mac insisted on my inspecting for the umpteenth time the collection of old handmade lures that he kept strictly for show. Carved out of cedar, bone, and perhaps an old walrus or elephant tusk—Mac wasn't sure—some of these primitive poppers and deep swimmers had been retired from their fish-catching duties for more than one hundred years. He also brought out an old, disassembled Calcutta cane rod and wiped its three shellacked sections shiny clean. I was reminded how much surfcasting equipment had changed once it was discovered that glass fibers could be bonded with synthetic resins.

"Better wear long johns under your waders," were Mac's parting words.

I also put two sweaters on under my foul-weather jacket and cut the right forefinger off an old pair of gloves to keep the mono from slipping off the tip of my finger when I threw open the bail. The big question then was, Where to go? The breakwater at Old Harbor or Southwest Point?

The answer was easy. On the breakwater at dawn, I would be casting directly into the rising sun. At Southwest Point at dusk I would casting into the setting sun before it slipped into the ocean. I always liked aiming my casts at the sun's red ball and then watching the plug swim back along a swath of sunlit sea. The iridescent water made the lure look more alive.

The breakwater at Old Harbor had some other attractions. Stripers are drawn to these man-made structures because of the silversides and eels that feed off the periwinkles, plankton, and other organic matter clinging to the stones. Also, casting distance isn't crucial from a breakwater. An eight-foot rod will get the plug out to where the stripers are feeding. The only difficulty is trying to land a fish from this high perch without using a long-handled gaff. It's best to tread backward along the top of the breakwater to the beach, carefully playing the fish all the way.

An onshore wind was buffeting the breakwater and blowing hard against my casts. It was still dark. The lights of a tanker headed for Providence crept across the horizon. This was the same horizon on which the pirate ships of Captain William Kidd and Joseph Bradish first hove into view three hundred years ago. Often when I see ships silhouetted there I think of those two swashbuckling buccaneers, both of whom are believed to have buried treasure on Block Island. It has been avidly searched for but never found.

Block had its own home-bred pirate, Paulsgrave Williams, who sailed with "Black Sam" Bellamy. Returning from the Caribbean with their plunder, the

two men planned to drop anchor where the breakwater is today, so Williams could visit his family. But
they missed the island in a storm. Their crew was said
to be on a "drunken spree" when on April 26, 1717,
their ship the *Whydah* crashed into a sandbar off Cape
Cod with its booty of silver and gold still aboard. A
scuba diver happened upon the wreck and its treasure
trove in 1984. Those treasures are still being recovered
and are now on permanent display at the Pilgrims'
Monument in Provincetown.

I never cared much for fishing from breakwaters or
jetties. I miss the feeling of being in the water together
with the fish. Obviously many of the other local fishermen don't share my prejudice and prefer staying dry.
One of the most popular surfcasting spots on the island is a long jetty known as the "pooper-scooper" because of the sewage discharge pipe that runs out into
the ocean beneath it. But I have assiduously avoided
the pooper-scooper, even though the nutrients spew-
ing from it into the water are said to attract schools
of baitfish.

After an hour of futile casts, I moved off the breakwater and onto the beach in front of Ballard's Inn.
The lifeguard's high perch hadn't yet been removed,
but the inn was boarded up for the winter, and the
beach was deserted.

Some very large bass are caught there during the
summer months. Many, I suspect, end up in the inn's
cavernous kitchen, which specializes in surf-and-turf

dinners and boasts of serving up some seven hundred lobsters every night. After closing time, the chefs often wander out on the beach to bargain for any freshly caught blues and bass.

Another hour of casting from the beach yielded only a few long strands of seaweed. But my hunter-gatherer instincts had shifted into high gear. I suddenly spotted in the crashing surf in front of me a sixty-pound leviathan lady bass so plump she could barely waddle through those big waves on her way to the Chesapeake, where next spring she would deposit half a million eggs and start a whole new generation of stripers. All I had to do was intercept her and she would be our Thanksgiving dinner. Much too big for our silver serving platter at home. Well, we'd just have to find something large enough to accommodate her. If only she'd pause on her travels and pounce on my new green plug posing as a mackerel.

The sun climbed out of the sea and into the sky. But the plug kept swimming back to me unscathed. "Could it be causing too much commotion in the water?" I asked myself. Maybe that big clunky thing was scaring rather than attracting any fish in the vicinity.

It's well known that a striper's lateral line, the mucus-filled channel lined with clusters of hairlike antennae, will pick up the vibrations of even the smallest lures from quite a distance. So I switched plugs, tying on a sleek yellow needlefish with a rubber sand-eel teaser that would skip over the surf ahead of it.

This big-fish-chasing-a-little-fish looked so enticing that even the most bloated bass with a stomach full of mossbunker could hardly resist it. Or so I thought. But during the next hour not one striper made even a halfhearted pass at either the plug or the teaser. Obviously, the time had come to head over to Bethany's Airport Diner for breakfast. If the fish weren't famished, I was.

A short stack with two sausages swimming in maple syrup revived my spirits enough that I made a brief stop for a few more casts at Black Rock. What made me think of trying this rugged surfcasting beach was some reminiscing by the breakfast crowd about the Portuguese passenger ship *Mormugao,* which had run aground there during Prohibition. The 450 passengers were rescued. But a crew of longshoremen summoned from Boston to remove the sand ballast and lighten the vessel so it could be towed out into deep water got fall-down drunk after discovering several hundred cases of whiskey buried in the ballast.

As one of the old-timers at Bethany's was saying: "Bringing booze to Block Island during Prohibition was like carrying coals to Newcastle."

The surf at Black Rock was so wild it almost knocked me down. Also, my needlefish with the teaser was being batted around so crazily I replaced it with a large Hopkins, heavy enough to reach beyond the breakers and to stay down in the less turbulent water near the bottom when I reeled it in. But all I caught was a seaweed-covered boulder hidden at high tide; it still has my Hopkins. Anyway, there was no sign of my Thanksgiving striper. So I drove back home to relax until late afternoon, when an incoming tide and fading light would make conditions perfect at Southwest Point.

By then the wind had dropped and the seas were calmer. Sometimes a sixth sense tells you when you're going to get a fish. It was with high anticipation that I pulled on my waders. They had been drying next to the furnace and were still warm, adding a sense of physical well-being to the positive feeling I had about catching a striper.

The sun was hovering just above the horizon, waiting to be extinguished by the sea—one of the likeliest moments for a striper to strike. Because they have no eyelids to protect them from the sun's penetration of the water, dusk is when stripers are drawn into the shallows to feed.

I could almost smell them. But that's not so crazy. Some surfcasters claim you actually can. One of my fishing buddies calls the smell "Eau de Morone"— a play on *Morone saxatilis,* the Latin name for striped bass.

Just as it does the bass, the edge of the sea tugs hardest at me at the end of the day. Especially when I'm just standing idly on the shore, not fishing or even thinking about fish. The last bright rim of light lining the horizon illuminates my soul. Yet when the sun drops a little lower and completely disappears, it moves me to unspeakable sadness, as if life itself, and not just the day, is ending.

Once again I tied on the big bottle-nosed plug. This time I added a strip of the supple pork rind to the back hook, giving the ungainly green lure a white, wiggly, come-hither tail. Then I sent it flying over the choppy sea, already tinged a deep orange. The plug hit the water with a splash, sending up almost as much spray as a leaping fish.

I had just started reeling when I saw what I thought was a slight swirl behind the plug. It was barely discernible, yet clear enough to make my heart skip a beat.

"Are you my Thanksgiving striper? Or is anticipation distorting my vision?"

I gave the plug a couple of quick jerks to simulate a wounded mackerel struggling to reach the safety of the shallows. Nothing happened. The plug continued to bounce back unmolested over the choppy surface.

As fast as I could, I sent it flying back to the same spot in the water where I'd seen the swirl. Before the plug even splashed down, the sea erupted. A shower of backlit spray flew into the air, and for a fleeting second I glimpsed dusky stripes stitched to silver scales. But the rod still felt light in my hands.

"Did that clumsy lunker miss my lure?"

A second later, fifty or sixty pounds of striped bass was pulling me forward with such force that I felt the soles of my waders sliding over the smooth, round stones that make surfcasting at Southwest Point so dangerous. Could a mere fish drag a grown man into the deep?

I loosened the drag. Line zipped off the reel with the sound of tearing paper as my Thanksgiving striper headed out to sea.

"No use trying to turn this big boy—or is it a girl?—around." I still had at least two hundred feet of mono left on the reel.

I had read of stripers having a "sinewed heart." Their courage and will to live was admired even by Block Island's Indians, who in their own threatened existence must have endured as much nearness to death as these fish. According to local lore the Indians also saw in these wild, leaping, lunging creatures the strength and exuberance for life they found in themselves.

The line was pulled so taut it started to hum, strummed by the wind that was picking up again. That sound is music to a surfcaster's ears.

I hadn't noticed that the waves, kicked up by the freshening wind, were now hitting well above the belt of my waders. Seawater gets heavier as it gets colder, but I was barely aware of the added pressure against my stomach and chest. But then it's well known that surfcasting holds the dubious distinction of being the least-comfortable form of fishing.

The powerful striper was still tugging hard, pulling me deeper into the water. Summoning all the strength left in my tired arms, I raised the rod, then quickly lowered it, reeling in the slack line created by the rod's sudden forward motion. That maneuver gained me a couple of feet of mono. Luckily, the striper didn't realize that for a brief second it probably had enough slack to shake the hook.

The sky was purpling fast. I wanted to bring this baby in before it became too dark and cold to gut and scale the fish on the beach. Unless, of course, it looked close to a record. In that case I'd have to barge in on Mac Swienton's supper and prevail upon the old man to open up the tackle shop and weigh it.

A sudden lunge and the fish veered to the left, swimming parallel to the shore. Even in the dim light I could see its dorsal fin cutting the water. It was moving fast, headed for the rocky point that might be its salvation. Swimming in and around the huge boulders it would probably succeed in shredding the tenuous twenty-pound test connecting me to him.

I backed up onto the beach and was able to follow the lumbering fish on foot, gaining a little line with each step. "He's finally tiring," I thought. But that foolish notion dissolved as the bass leapt half out of the sea, baring a broad brown back, and then dove for the bottom, taking all my regained mono with him.

"Be patient," I reminded myself. "Don't try to horse this fellow in. Wait for the lactic acid buildup in its muscles to sap its strength."

But that wasn't happening. Instead, it was my

muscles that were aching. The striper seemed stronger than ever, keeping my rod doubled over, sometimes dunking the tip into the water.

Would I still be fighting this monster when the moon peeked over the cliff behind me? The duel would have then turned into an endurance contest that could go on for an hour, or even longer. By that time I'd be whipped, though the fish probably wouldn't.

An observation once made by Joseph Conrad flashed through my mind: "The sea has never been friendly to man. At most it has been the accomplice of human restlessness."

Surfcasting, I've known for a long time, is the best outlet for my restlessness. Usually it matters little whether or not I catch something. The quest itself provides a path to the solace that's so difficult to find. But hubris was suddenly entering into my fight with this striper, seizing me with an almost angry, must-win feeling that I'd never felt toward a fish before.

It wasn't simply my whim to serve a Thanksgiving striper that was goading me to slay this fish. I was finally experiencing the primeval urge that leads meat fishermen to measure success entirely by their ability to kill and bring home their quarry.

Perhaps I hadn't realized how this fall's striper migration had sent the blood coursing through me with the same energy as the vast schools moving south. I had become determined to catch and keep one of these lunkers. And now hooked up to possibly the last bass of the season, there was no way it was going to go free.

Lost in these thoughts, I didn't notice the line dribbling off my reel until I looked down and saw there was little left. I waded back into the water, cranking hard to gain line but finding no firm footing on the slippery stones. And suddenly there I was flat on my behind on the rocky bottom, with water pouring into my waders.

Before I could scramble back up on my feet, the fish reappeared on top, furiously shaking its head, trying to dislodge the plug. I watched it bobbing and weaving like a boxer ducking a flurry of punches— only the painful jabs were not coming directly from me, but from hard jerks on the big wooden plug sticking out of its enormous mouth, cavernous enough, I was sure, to belong to a sixty-pounder.

"At least it's well hooked. But will its razor-sharp pectorals slice through my mono?" As usual, I hadn't put on a leader. This time I wished I had.

My thoughts were again turning to Thanksgiving when without warning the thrashing at the other end of the mono stopped and the line went limp. The end had come so unexpectedly I didn't know whether to curse or cry. Perhaps I did both. I was in such a daze I don't remember.

Reeling in the line, I watched the big green plug coming toward me, bouncing as carelessly and seductively over the surface chop as if it had never been attacked.

Any other time I might have felt exhilarated by the sheer excitement of having done battle with such a strong and wily animal, even though it won and I lost. I might have actually conceded that it deserved the victory, or rationalized my defeat as a gain for conservation. But this time I was mad. So mad I nearly hurled my rod and reel into the ocean.

It was almost dark. Not until I was back on the beach ready to leave did I notice that the plug's back hook—the one with the strip of Uncle Josh pork rind hanging from it—was gone. The whole hook and connecting ring had been ripped clean out of the plug's wooden body, attesting to that striper's extraordinary strength.

Or was it a flaw in that clunky plug's construction? Sure, I could write an irate letter to the manufacturer. But that's no consolation for losing a magnificent striper.

I suppose you could say there *was* one consolation. At least I had a good fish story to tell our assembled guests on Thanksgiving Day as they exclaimed over the plump thirty-pound turkey I was carving.

"Somewhere between Block Island and the Chesapeake Bay," I said, "there's a much bigger bird swimming south with a hook in its mouth to remember me by."